SPECTRUM®

Reading

Grade 3

Spectrum®
An imprint of Carson-Dellosa Publishing LLC
P.O. Box 35665
Greensboro, NC 27425 USA

ISBN 978-0-7696-3863-8

14-188147811

Index of Skills

Reading Grade 3

Numerals indicate the exercise pages on which these skills appear.

Vocabulary Skills

Abbreviations 33, 61, 93, 103, 133

Antonyms 9, 27, 53, 65, 77, 91, 105, 123, 139

Base Words and Endings 3, 19, 35, 39, 47, 69, 85, 105, 119, 141

Classification 7, 23, 39, 51, 67, 81, 101, 119, 135

Compound Words 11, 27, 43, 63, 75, 101, 115, 143

Contractions 23, 39, 81, 91, 117, 139, 147

Homographs 15, 45, 59, 97, 119

Homophones 15, 31, 45, 55, 75, 107, 137, 149

Irregular Spellings 31, 73, 97, 121, 141

Meaning From Context 3, 7, 11, 19, 21, 29, 37, 41, 43, 47, 49, 53, 55, 61, 65, 71, 73, 79, 81, 85, 89, 95, 101, 105, 109, 121, 127, 131, 137, 147

Multiple Meanings 25, 35, 89, 103, 129

Multisyllabic Words 5, 49, 73, 107, 127, 147

Possessives 21, 47, 69, 87, 111, 123, 145

Prefixes and Suffixes 9, 19, 43, 63, 79, 107, 115, 125, 151

r-Controlled Vowels 17, 37, 51, 71, 95, 115, 131, 145

Singular and Plural 3, 25, 45, 59, 79, 109, 117, 135, 151

Syllables 13, 29, 57, 77, 99, 113, 133, 149

Synonyms 5, 21, 41, 71, 93, 111, 129, 145

Variant Sounds 27, 49, 67, 113, 129, 141

Vowel Digraphs and Diphthongs 17, 33, 57, 83, 111, 125, 143

Reading Skills

Cause and Effect 11, 13, 31, 45, 61, 95, 111, 129, 151

Character Analysis 5, 23, 25, 53, 75, 91, 105, 127, 137

Comparison and Contrast 19, 21, 51, 73, 97, 109, 125, 127, 143

Context Clues 11, 23, 43, 51, 57, 81, 93, 107, 117, 139, 149

Drawing Conclusions 3, 17, 31, 41, 47, 61, 67, 85, 101, 113, 131, 145

Fact and Opinion 17, 39, 49, 59, 83, 101, 115, 135, 147

Facts and Details 3, 9, 15, 19, 27, 37, 47, 55, 57, 73, 95, 105, 115, 135, 143, 147

Give Purpose for Reading *all*

Identify Author's Purpose 13, 39, 77, 83, 117, 139

Main Idea 3, 9, 19, 29, 37, 47, 55, 73, 79, 95, 105, 115, 139, 147

Predicting Outcomes 3, 25, 35, 41, 51, 79, 97, 107, 119, 145

Reality and Fantasy 15, 35, 53, 71, 81, 99, 111, 141

Recognize Features of Familiar Genres, Including Stories, Informational Text, etc. 5, 27, 49, 59, 65, 85, 99, 117, 123, 151

Recognize Story's Problem 29, 45, 63, 71, 107

Sequence 7, 17, 33, 69, 87, 99, 103, 129, 133, 151

Show Comprehension by Identifying Answers in Text 15, 33, 45, 59, 75, 89, 109, 137

Understand and Identify Simple Literature Terms (e.g., author, illustrator, dialogue, etc.) 29, 39, 43, 63, 89, 111, 131

Use Prior Knowledge 5, 21, 41, 67, 73, 91, 107, 113, 133, 143

Word Referents 13, 43, 69, 87, 101, 137, 149

Study Skills

Alphabetical Order 9, 41, 75, 87, 117, 131, 143, 149

Dictionary Use 11, 55, 65, 91, 113, 127

Following Directions *all*

Interpret Information Diagrams, Graphs, Charts 7, 27, 61, 77, 93, 109, 125

Parts of a Book 57, 103, 123

Reference Materials 67, 83, 95, 121, 141

Use Titles, TOC, Headings, Glossaries, Indexes to Locate Information 13, 21, 37, 61, 67, 85, 109, 121, 125

Table of Contents

Two Boys, Big Plans 2
One Tent, Lots of Stuff. 4
How to Pitch a Tent 6
One Tent...What Next? 8
Night Lights 10
Thunder and Lightning 12
Smokey the Bear. 14
Planting Dreams 16
Dreaming of the Harvest 18
Peppers. 20
The Pie Man 22
Once a Pie Man, Always a Pie Man 24
New York City's Gem. 26
Soccer Blues 28
Mom to the Rescue. 30
Power Snack 32
And It's Out of the Park! 34
History of Soccer. 36
Why Soccer? 38
A Teacher's Journal. 40
A Student's Journal 42
The Great Volcano Debate 44
The End of a Volcano Tale 46
Volcanoes 48
And the Next Unit Is. 50
So Many Ideas 52
Too Many Ideas! 54
Forest Mammals 56
Snakes: Love Them or Leave Them? . . . 58
Redwood Giants 60
Problem Solved 62
The Hamster From Room 144 64
Caring for a Pet Hamster 66
Skyway Sweeper. 68
Rooftop Keeper 70
The Dirt on Soil 72
Frederick's Secret 74
Buildings: From Tall to Taller 76
Magic With Flowers. 78
Magic With Wiggles. 80
Houdini 82
David Copperfield 84
Wiggles Reappears. 86
Field Trip 88
Riddles Along the Way 90
One Great Wall 92

A Wall of Names 94
A Farm From Long Ago 96
In the Barn. 98
In the Kitchen 100
Baking Bread. 102
All About the Farm. 104
Caught in Traffic 106
How Many Are There?. 108
Sidewalk Art. 110
Wishes on the Sidewalk 112
Drawings on the Wall. 114
Roman Wall Art 116
From Lucy 118
At the Shore 120
From Isabel 122
The Dominican Republic. 124
Lucy and Isabel: Pen Pals. 126
Phone Troubles 128
Phone Manners 130
Hold the Phone!. 132
Telephones: How Do They Work?. . . . 134
Honey to the Rescue. 136
Honey 138
A Sad Song 140
What Is Folk Music? 142
Peanut Butter Plus 144
Working for Peanuts 146
All Wrapped Up 148
Making Prints. 150
Answer Key 152

Two Boys, Big Plans

Read to see what Sam and Kent are planning.

1   "Okay, I'm going to ask my parents right now. Are you?" Sam waited for Kent's reply over the phone.

2   "I think so," said Kent after a moment. "My dad just got home a little while ago. Are you bringing crackers?"

3   Sam laughed. Kent was always hungry. "Yes, I'll bring the crackers," he said. "And be sure to tell them that we'll turn the lights out by 9:30. Okay?"

4   "Nine-thirty. Right," Kent agreed. "Okay, I'm going to go ask. I'll talk to you in a little bit."

5   "Okay," answered Sam, and he hung up. *Now, if only we can talk our parents into letting us do this*, he thought to himself. He put on a big smile and entered the family room.

6   "Dad?" said Sam quietly so he wouldn't make his father jump. "I cleaned up those grass clippings for you."

7   "Oh, good," nodded Mr. Hume. "Thanks, Sam."

8   "Mom? Dad?" started Sam again. Both his parents looked over their newspapers. The words rushed out of Sam. "Kent and I were wondering if we could sleep out in the tent tonight. We'd be warm enough in our sleeping bags, and we won't eat too much, and it'll be lights out at 9:30, we promise."

9   Mr. and Mrs. Hume blinked, then looked at each other. *How do they talk to each other without saying anything*, wondered Sam.

10   "Did Kent's parents say it was okay?" asked Mrs. Hume.

11   "He's asking right now." Sam shifted from one foot to the other. Another look passed between his parents.

12   Mr. Hume nodded. "If Kent's parents say it's okay, it's okay with us."

13   "Thanks, Dad! Thanks, Mom!" called Sam as he dashed for the phone. He dialed and held his breath. Then, he heard Kent's voice.

14   "Okay?" asked Sam.

15   "Okay!" said Kent.

Vocabulary Skills

Write the words from the story that have these meanings.

1. answer

   reply <small>Par. 1</small>

2. inquire

   ask <small>Par. 4</small>

3. went into

   letting <small>Par. 5</small>

4. went quickly

   _____ <small>Par. 8</small>

A word without an ending is a **base** word. Circle the base word in each of the words below.

5. bringing   6. lights

7. quietly   8. blinked

A word that names one of something is **singular**. A word that names more than one is **plural**. Most words are made plural by adding an **s** at the end. Write the plural form of these words.

9. cracker ___crackers___

10. parent ___parents___

11. tent ___tents___

12. word ___words___

Reading Skills

1. This story is mostly about

   _____ a sleepover.

   _____ Sam's parents.

   __✓__ two boys' plans.

2. At the beginning, when Sam and Kent are talking on the phone, what did you think they might be talking about?

   They might be talking

   _____

3. In the story, when did you find out what the boys are planning?

   In paragraph 8.

   _____

4. Why do you think Sam told his dad about the grass clippings?

   He would get a reward
   ford chore

   _____

5. Why does Sam mention being warm enough and when the lights will be turned out?

   So sams parents
   will know that he'll be

6. Now that the boys have permission, what do you think they will do next?

   They'll get up theyre
   tent

One Tent, Lots of Stuff

What do the boys need for their night in the tent?

1 "Lantern?"

2 "Got it."

3 "Sleeping bags?"

4 "Got it—both of them."

5 "Pillows?"

6 "Two fat ones."

7 "Crackers?"

8 "Three kinds."

9 "Three kinds? Great!"

10 Sam and Kent had made a list of all the things they needed for sleeping out in the tent. Now, they were sitting cross-legged in the tent, checking things off the list.

11 "Are you going to bring a bathrobe and slippers?" Kent asked Sam.

12 "Oh, no! We're camping. Those are just for in the house," answered Sam, looking as if he knew all about camping.

13 "Oh, right," said Kent, who had never been camping before. He didn't think Sam had been camping before either. Still, it was Sam's dad's tent, so he must know.

14 "Oh, I almost forgot. Can you bring your baseball glove?" Sam looked very serious.

15 Kent couldn't figure this one out. "My baseball glove? What do we need that for?"

16 "Well, we just might. You never know," said Sam with mystery and authority.

17 "Okay," shrugged Kent, "I'll bring it when I come after supper. What time do you think you'll be able to come out?"

18 Sam thought for a moment. "We usually eat at 5:45. Then, I have to clear the table. I should be done by 6:30. What about you?"

19 "My dad doesn't get home until six o'clock," said Kent, regretfully. "Maybe if I offer to help Mom with supper, things will go quickly."

20 Sam shrugged. "It's worth a try. Come out as soon as you can." Sam looked around the tent. "Okay, I think everything's ready. I'll see you later."

21 "See you later," said Kent, and the boys both ran home.

Vocabulary Skills

Words that mean the same, or nearly the same, are called **synonyms**. Circle the pair of synonyms in each row.

1. (many) fat all (countless)
2. (serious) narrow (unsmiling) busy
3. special (after) (moment) instant
4. (shortly) later (soon) gladly
5. helpful finished glum done

Each word part is called a **syllable**. The words below are broken into syllables. Sound out each syllable. Then, write the word and say it to yourself as you write.

6. mys/ter/y _mystery_

7. au/thor/i/ty _authority_

8. re/gret/ful/ly _regretfully_

Reading Skills

1. One of the boys usually has the ideas. The other one seems to go along with those ideas. Which boy is the "leader"? _SAM_

2. What details from the story helped you answer question 1?

_____

3. Kent says he might help his mom with supper. What does that tell you about Kent?

_____
_____
_____

4. Based on what you know about camping, how do you feel about all the stuff the boys have in their tent? List what you think they need and what they don't need.

What They Need

_____
_____
_____

What They Don't Need

_____
_____
_____

5. In some stories, the author tells you what is happening. In this story, the author uses mostly **dialogue**, what the characters say, to let you know what is going on. Choose one line of dialogue and write what it helps you know about the character.

Dialogue: _____

_____
_____
_____

How to Pitch a Tent

Follow these instructions to learn how to pitch a tent.

These general instructions should allow anyone to pitch any size or style of tent. Keep in mind that pitching a tent alone, even if you have experience, is difficult.

1. Choose a flat area on which to pitch your tent. Remove any stones or rocks that might poke through the tent's floor.

2. Take the tent and all equipment out of the storage bag. Lay everything on the ground neatly.

3. Spread a groundcloth over the chosen spot. Then, lay the tent floor, over the groundcloth. Fold the edges of the groundcloth under, so they do not stick out from the edges of the tent.

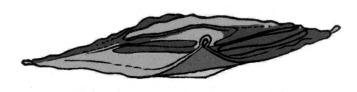

4. Make sure the tent door is zipped shut. Then, pound a stake through each loop, pulling snugly as you go so the floor gets stretched to its full size.

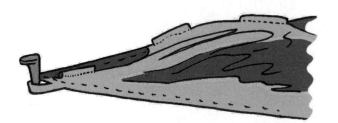

5. Put together the tent poles, if necessary. Thread each one through its loops or channels. Do not step or walk on the tent to do this. If necessary, crawl or lie down on your stomach to reach the center of the tent.

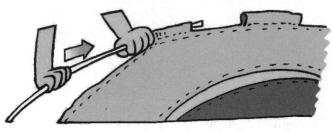

6. Raise the poles. If you have a partner, work on opposite sides of the tent.

7. Pull the guy lines straight out from the sides of the tent. Peg each one.

Vocabulary Skills

Write the words from the article that have these meanings.

1. to push through

   <u>POKIE</u>  _{Step 1}

2. with care and order

   <u>heatly</u> _{Step 2} X

3. to strike heavily

   <u>powhd</u> _{Step 4}

4. middle or interior point

   <u>Center</u> _{Step 5}

In each row below, circle the three words that belong together.

5. grass (stones   rocks) (pebbles)

6. (set   lay) (put) jet

7. (tight) windy (snug) (stretched)

8. (haul) (pull) snap (heave)

Reading Skills

1. What do you know about pitching a tent? Do you have anything to add to these instructions?

   <u>Go inside the</u>
   <u>tent and sleep.</u>

2. Number the sentences to show the order to pitch a tent.

   _3_ Spread out groundcloth.

   _7_ Tighten and peg guy lines.

   _1_ Choose and clear an area.

   _6_ Put together tent poles.

   _2_ Lay out equipment.

   _4_ Pound stakes through loops.

   _6_ Raise the poles.

Study Skills

1. If you don't know or understand what a guy line is, which illustration helps you figure it out? Tell how.

   _____
   _____
   _____
   _____
   _____

2. Choose one illustration. Explain what it shows.

   <u>The fourth</u>
   <u>step shows a</u>
   <u>tent flat on the</u>
   <u>floor.</u>

One Tent...What Next?

What do the boys expect to happen?

1   "Then, there was the time my brother and I nearly got blown away with the tent! Did I tell you about that one?" Sam shook his head and tried not to look impatient. His dad had been telling camping stories for almost an hour. *How can I get him to stop without saying anything?* thought Sam to himself. He really wanted to get out to the tent.

2   Finally, his dad stopped for a bite of dessert, and Sam asked to be excused. When his mom nodded her okay, it took only four trips to clear the table. Then, he was off and across the backyard.

3   "Caught you!" yelled Sam as he flipped back the tent flap. Kent jumped and turned red. "Ha! I knew it! In the crackers already." Then, he laughed. "Have you been waiting long?"

4   Kent shook his head because his mouth was full. Finally, he said, "Not long. My dad got home late."

5   Sam shrugged. "Oh, well. We're here now. Let's get ready."

6   "Ready for what?" asked Kent.

7   "For whatever's going to happen," answered Sam. *Well, he must know,* thought Kent. He helped Sam straighten the sleeping bags and stash stuff in the corners. They played catch across the tent for a little while. *Ah, the baseball glove,* thought Kent. They played badminton with crackers, but then Sam discovered crumbs in his sleeping bag, so they stopped.

8   They turned on the lantern and read. After a while, Sam retold some of his dad's camping stories. Then, Kent turned out the light, and they listened for noises in the dark. They didn't hear any for a very long time.

9   Finally, Kent heard something at the tent flap. He half crawled and half flew across the tent to warn Sam. Sam yelled when Kent landed on top of him.

10   "Hey, are you guys all right?" It was Sam's mom. "Breakfast is ready."

11   Sam and Kent looked at each other in disbelief. They had slept through the whole night, and nothing had happened.

Vocabulary Skills

Words whose meanings are opposite are called **antonyms**. Match each word in the first list with its antonym in the second list. Write the letter in the blank.

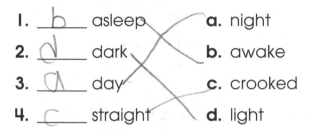

1. __b__ asleep   **a.** night
2. __d__ dark   **b.** awake
3. __a__ day   **c.** crooked
4. __c__ straight   **d.** light

A **prefix** is a group of letters added to the beginning of a word that changes the meaning of a word.

The prefix **re-** means "again."

- *retold* means "told again"

The prefix **im-** means "not."

- *impatient* means "not patient"

Write the correct word next to its meaning.

impolite	reappear
impossible	refill

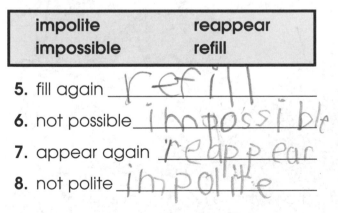

5. fill again __refill__
6. not possible __impossible__
7. appear again __reappear__
8. not polite __impolite__

Reading Skills

1. Which sentence best describes this story?

_____ Nothing exciting happens to the boys in the tent.

___a___ The boys have a crazy night in the tent.

_____ In the morning, Kent plays a trick on Sam and scares him.

2. Why did the boys stop playing badminton?

__Sam discovered crumbs in his sleeping bag__

Study Skills

Number each list of words below in alphabetical order.

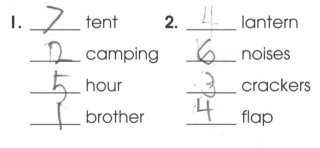

1. __7__ tent   2. __4__ lantern
   __2__ camping   __6__ noises
   __5__ hour   __3__ crackers
   __1__ brother   __4__ flap

Night Lights

What is keeping Mikki awake?

1   There were lights flashing outside. No matter what I did, I could see those lights. I couldn't figure out what they were, so I started worrying.

2   I turned away from the window and closed my eyes. But then I had to open them, just a crack, to see if the lights were still there. *Flash-flash, off, flash!*

3   I rolled toward the window and watched. Maybe I could figure it out. I started listing things. Car lights? Not bright enough. Police car flashers? Not blue and red enough. Space ships? Not likely. All right, this is really bugging me. I have to go ask Mom, I finally concluded.

4   I padded downstairs where my mom was reading a magazine. She was a little surprised to see me.

5   "The lights are flashing upstairs," I said.

6   "They are?" She said it with that "this is a great excuse for being out of bed" look on her face.

7   "I can't figure out what it is," I continued, hoping for some comfort. To my relief, she put down her magazine and steered me back upstairs.

8   We laid across my bed on our stomachs and watched out the window. Mom knew right away.

9   "Mikki, do you remember driving up to visit Uncle Walt last month?" she asked. I nodded. "Do you remember how long it took?" I nodded again. "Well, Uncle Walt is having a thunderstorm way up north where his house is. The lightning is sort of shining off the clouds, so we can see the flashing down here, even though the storm is far away from us."

10   "Oh," I said. I thought to myself, *Well, that makes sense.* After all, what else causes lights to flash in the sky? Aliens? Not likely.

Vocabulary Skills

Write the words from the story that have these meanings.

1. light appearing in brief bursts

_____
Par. 1

2. feeling anxious or upset

_____
Par. 1

3. reason

_____
Par. 6

4. relief from worry

_____
Par. 7

A **compound word** is made by combining two smaller words. Use the underlined words in each sentence to form a compound word. Write the word in the blank.

5. A room that is <u>down</u> the <u>stairs</u> is

_____.

6. A <u>storm</u> that includes <u>thunder</u> is a

_____.

Reading Skills

1. What is causing Mikki to worry?

_____

2. What does Mikki do to try to get to sleep?

First, she _____

_____.

Then, she _____

_____.

3. What is causing the flashing lights?

_____

_____

_____

4. Have you ever been kept awake at night by something that bothered or puzzled you? Write about it.

_____

_____

_____

_____

Study Skills

Each word you look up in a dictionary is called an **entry word**. Most entry words are base words. That is, they don't have endings. So, to look up the word *worrying*, you should find the base word *worry*. Write the correct entry word in each blank.

To Look Up	Find the Entry Word
1. rolled	_____
2. watched	_____
3. listing	_____
4. flashing	_____
5. continued	_____

Thunder and Lightning

What causes thunder and lightning?

1 The story of thunder and lightning is a lesson on electricity. Lightning is really just a giant electrical spark. Thunder is a direct result of the activity of that spark.

Lightning First

2 Imagine a single water droplet high above Earth. It is in a cloud among millions of other water droplets. As this water droplet falls toward Earth, it gets bigger by collecting more moisture. When the droplet gets to just about the size of a pea, it splits. This splitting action causes an electrical charge to build up on the two new droplets.

3 If the droplets fall straight to Earth, the electrical charge is very small and will have no effect. If the droplets get swept upward by air currents, however, the whole process begins again. The droplets fall, grow, split, and become more strongly charged with electricity each time.

4 In time, the electrical charge in the droplets becomes so strong that it has to discharge itself. The result is a huge spark. It may leap from a cloud to the ground in less than one-tenth of a second. We know it as lightning.

Thunder Second

5 When lightning flashes, the air is suddenly heated, then it quickly cools. These rapid changes in the air cause the cracking sound of thunder. During a storm, we see lightning first, then wait to hear the thunder. That's because light travels faster than sound. We see the lightning as it happens, but the sound of the thunder may take any number of seconds to reach us, depending on how far away the lightning was. The rumbling sound of thunder is actually an echo from the sound waves bouncing off Earth or off the clouds.

Vocabulary Skills

A word part is called a **syllable**. When a word has two consonants between two vowels, the syllables are divided between the two consonants. For example, *number* is divided like this: *num / ber*.

For each word below, draw a line to divide the word into syllables.

1. d r o p/l e t
2. e f/f e c t
3. c u r/r e n t s
4. f a s/t e r
5. h a p/p e n s

Reading Skills

1. The author wrote this article to

    _____ entertain.

    __√__ give information.

    _____ persuade.

2. Which comes first, thunder or lightning?

    lightning

3. What causes lightning? Give a brief answer.

    The electricity in a
    water droplet.

4. How does lightning cause thunder?

    Lightning creates(heat)changes
    in the air which make
    sound.

Words such as *he, she, you, it,* and *them* are called **pronouns**. They are used in place of other nouns. Read this sentence:

> Ty heard thunder when he woke up.

In the sentence, *he* stands for *Ty.* Now, read each sentence below. Fill in the blank.

5. When the droplet gets too big, it splits.

    It stands for _the droplet_.

6. Lynn ran for cover, but she got wet anyway.

    She stands for _Lynn_.

7. The girls thought they saw lightning.

    They stands for _the girls_.

Study Skills

1. If you read only the two headings in this article, what would you learn?

    Lighting come, then
    thunder.

Smokey the Bear

Read to find out how Smokey the Bear became famous.

1   Smokey the Bear's story doesn't start with a bear. It starts with a problem, a solution, and then a drawing.

2   In the 1940s, during World War II, the leaders of the United States had a problem. They were worried about having enough wood to build ships and other equipment for the war. The solution: To protect America's forests (and the wood that might be needed for ships), the U.S. Forest Service started a campaign to prevent forest fires.

3   The Forest Service created posters reminding people about fire safety. The posters featured a deer named Bambi from a popular movie. Before long, however, the poster images were switched to a popular toy animal—a bear. An illustrator, Albert Staehle, drew that first bear with a park ranger's hat in 1944 and named him *Smokey*.

4   Six years later, while fighting a forest fire in New Mexico, firefighters found a black bear cub clinging to a tree. They rescued the cub and called it Hotfoot. Soon, however, the cub was renamed Smokey after the drawings on the posters.

5   Once he recovered from his injuries, Smokey was taken to the National Zoo in Washington, D.C. Thousands of people visited him there until he died in 1976. Smokey was 26 years old. His message is still with us, however, as we see him reminding us to prevent forest fires all across the nation.

Vocabulary Skills

Homophones are words that sound alike but have different spellings and different meanings. Complete each sentence below by writing the correct word in the blank.

1. Smokey the ___Bear___ is easy to recognize. (Bare, Bear)

2. The ___wood___ in our forests is valuable. (wood, would)

Homographs are words that are spelled the same but have different meanings. For example, *bat* can name a stick used in baseball or a flying mammal. Choose the correct word below to complete each pair of sentences.

park	ships

3. The ___ships___ were lined up in the harbor.

   Grandma always ___ships___ a package for my birthday.

4. I looked for a place to ___park___ the car.

   We had a picnic in the ___park___.

Reading Skills

Put a check next to the sentences that are true.

1. __✓__ The idea for Smokey the Bear started in the 1940s.

2. _____ Smokey the Bear lives in New Mexico.

3. _____ The Forest Service made posters in honor of a bear cub that died in a fire.

4. __✓__ Smokey the Bear was a drawing first, then a real bear.

Write **M** next to the sentences that tell about make-believe things.

5. _____ Smokey the Bear lived in a zoo for many years.

6. __M__ Smokey the Bear speaks to campers about the danger of forest fires.

7. __M__ Smokey the Bear used to help firefighters put out fires.

8. Why was Smokey the Bear created? Write the phrase or sentence from the article that tells you.

   ___To protect americas forests___

Planting Dreams

What does Rosa dream about?

1   She was walking home from work one evening when she got the idea. Rosa didn't like her job at the factory, but it was better than no job at all. So, while she was trying not to think about work, she saw the pots stacked up in an alley. They were cheap plastic pots, but there were dozens of them piled up behind the flower shop. Such a waste, she thought. When the pots were still there three days later, Rosa went in and asked if she could take some. The flower shop lady said she didn't mind, so Rosa carried home a tower of pots, pretending she was a circus performer on the way.

2   At home, Rosa set them on the fire escape outside her tiny apartment. And there they sat. Once a gust of wind sent them clattering to the street three floors below, and she had to go and chase them before the gathering storm.

3   Every day, Rosa went to work and thought about her pots. She was waiting for something, but she had patience.

4   At last, the newspaper brought good news. A hardware store had a sale on potting soil. Rosa carefully counted her money, then walked the six blocks to the store. She bought six bags and carried them home. She bought seeds, too. Rosa slept well that night and dreamed of masses of flowers and fat, glowing fruits.

5   Sundays were always good days. Rosa didn't have to work on Sundays. But Rosa couldn't remember when she had had *such* a good Sunday. She got up early and ate her breakfast on the fire escape with her pots. Then, she began to scoop dirt into the pots. She hummed a little song until all six of her bags of soil were empty. Then, she laid her precious seed packets out and planned her garden. Tomatoes for the biggest pots, and peppers for the next-biggest ones. Flowers in all the rest.

6   At the end of the day, Rosa sat in her garden and watched the sunset. *Soon*, she thought, *there will be masses of flowers and fat, glowing fruits.*

Vocabulary Skills

Circle the correct letters to complete each word. Write the letters in the blank.

1. The pots were behind the flow_____ shop.

       ir   er   ur

2. Rosa planted a g_____den in the pots.

       ar   or   er

3. She sat on the f_____e escape and watched the plants grow.

       ur   ir   er

4. Rosa dashed up the stairs to her ap_____tment.

       er   ar   ir

The missing words in these sentences contain the letters **ee** or **ea**. Fill in the blanks.

5. Rosa waited for _____ days before she asked about the pots.

6. She fell asleep and _____ about her garden.

7. It didn't matter that the pots were _____ and plastic.

8. Rosa planted _____ in her pots.

Reading Skills

A **fact** is something that can be proven true. An **opinion** is what someone thinks or feels. Check the sentences that are facts.

1. _____ Vegetables can be grown in pots.

2. _____ Creating a garden on a fire escape is difficult.

3. _____ Any garden is beautiful.

4. _____ Plants need soil and water.

5. Number the sentences to show the order in which things happened.

   _____ Rosa bought potting soil.

   _____ Rosa took the pots home.

   _____ Rosa planted her seeds.

   _____ Rosa saw the pots.

6. Check the words or phrases that best describe Rosa.

   _____ selfish

   _____ tends to waste time

   _____ likes the outdoors

   _____ appreciates beauty

Dreaming of the Harvest

Read to see how Rosa's garden is doing.

1   Rosa hurried home from work. She knew it had been quite warm that day, and it hadn't rained since last week. She was worried that her tiny seedlings might have gotten too much sun. When she got to her building, she raced up the stairs, two at a time, up to the third floor.

2   Rosa was still panting when she stepped out onto the fire escape. *Oh, you poor things!* was all she could think. Even her strongest, tallest tomato plant looked as if it had just given up. It was pale and dry looking, not green and smooth like it had been this morning. Rosa got her watering can and went right to work. She watered each pot until it began to drip out the holes in the bottom. She made sure each plant got just the right amount. Then, she went in to fix something to eat.

3   In the kitchen, Rosa bit into an apple and imagined that it was a big, juicy tomato. She chopped a carrot and imagined that it was a shiny, green pepper getting ready to join some tomatoes in a pot of rich, spicy sauce.

4   She carried her dinner out to the fire escape. The apartment building across the street cast its shadow on her garden, letting it rest from the day's hot sun. Rosa leaned against the wall and closed her eyes. She let her hard day of work at the factory fade away as she imagined taking her flowers to her friends at work. Just think how surprised they would be. They would think she had robbed the flower shop!

5   Rosa watched her garden grow until after dark. Then, she went inside and dreamed of running her own shop filled with trays of fresh vegetables and baskets of flowers fresh from her own garden.

Vocabulary Skills

Write the words from the story that have these meanings.

1. young plants

   _____
   Par. 1

2. breathing hard

   _____
   Par. 2

3. not rough

   _____
   Par. 2

A word without an ending is a **base** word. Circle the base word in each of the words below.

4. landing   5. watered

6. chopped   7. flowers

8. baskets

The suffix **-est** means "most." So, *tallest* means "most tall." Add the suffix **-est** to each word to change its meaning.

9. strong _____

10. high _____

Reading Skills

1. Why is Rosa worried about her plants on this day?

   _____

   _____

Write **T** if the sentence is true. Write **F** if the sentence is false.

2. _____ This story is mostly about Rosa worrying about her garden.

3. _____ Rosa is careless about her garden.

4. _____ Rosa plans to share her flowers with others.

5. _____ Too much sun causes Rosa's plants to dry up.

Compare how things really are with how they used to be, or with what Rosa imagines.

6. The strongest, tallest tomato plant is

   _____.

   It had been

   _____.

7. Rosa bites into an

   _____.

   She imagines that it is a

   _____.

8. She chops a

   _____.

   She imagines that it is a

   _____.

9. For now, Rosa works at a

   _____.

   She dreams of

   _____

   _____.

Peppers

Which kind of pepper do you like best?

1   What comes in many colors and is high in vitamins A and C? Some people like them hot; some prefer them mild. They are a common sight in backyard gardens throughout the United States. Have you guessed yet? They are peppers.

2   Whether green, yellow, or red, peppers add flavor to many types of foods. People eat them raw, pickled, or cooked. They go in salads, in sauces, on sandwiches, and, of course, on pizza.

Bell Peppers

3   The mildest variety of peppers is the bell pepper. They are sometimes called *sweet peppers*, but they are not sweet like sugar. They are simply less spicy, or hot, than other types of peppers. The round, apple-sized fruits of bell pepper plants are green, yellow, or red. Some people eat them before they get fully ripe. Bell peppers are by far the most common pepper found in gardens and on grocery store shelves.

Chili Peppers

4   "Chili pepper" is a general name for a number of quite spicy peppers that come in many sizes and appear red, yellow, or green. These hotter peppers tend to be long and skinny. Chili peppers don't actually burn your mouth, but they can cause pain. A certain chemical in the fruit causes this feeling. Chili peppers, whether fresh or dried, add an almost fiery zing to foods. Dishes from Mexico, India, and Africa are noted for including the hottest types of peppers. Eating these foods may take some getting used to. In addition to the discomfort in your mouth, hot peppers may cause your eyes to water, your nose to run, and your ears to feel warm.

5   Whatever their color or flavor, peppers add variety and spice to fancy or even everyday foods. When was the last time you had a pepper?

Vocabulary Skills

Write the words from the article that have these meanings.

1. gentle; not strong

   _____
   Par. 1

2. taste

   _____
   Par. 2

3. usual

   _____
   Par. 3

4. just harvested

   _____
   Par. 4

Synonyms are words that have the same or nearly the same meaning. Circle the two words that are synonyms in each row.

5. fresh   hot   spicy   green

6. raw   mild   uncooked   salad

7. red   cooked   sweet   sugary

To show that something belongs to someone, add **'s** to the end of a word. Complete each sentence. Use **'s** at the end of each person's name.

8. This cookbook belongs to Dad.
   It is _____ cookbook.

9. This frying pan belongs to Mom.
   It is _____ frying pan.

10. Sharon cooked this hot food.
    It is _____ hot food.

Reading Skills

1. What do you know about peppers, or what experiences have you had growing or eating peppers?

   _____

   _____

   _____

2. Do you like peppers? Write why or why not.

   _____

   _____

3. How are bell peppers and chili peppers the same? How are they different? Write what the article tells you about each kind.

   Bell Peppers

   Size _____

   Shape _____

   Color _____

   Flavor _____

   Chili Peppers

   Size _____

   Shape _____

   Color _____

   Flavor _____

The Pie Man

Read to see what Mr. Fellini remembers about his career.

1   Joseph Fellini waited for the light to change. Even early in the morning, Central Park South was busy and noisy. He knew that just across the street in the park, it would be quiet and pleasant. *Some things don't change,* he thought with a sigh.

2   When Joseph was a young man, people didn't realize how important it was to go to college. All that Joseph had wanted at age 17 was to get a job to help make sure he and his parents had food to eat. Food was what steered him to the bakery, he figured. It always smelled so good. He walked three blocks out of his way on the way home from high school just to smell it. Then, one May day, there was a sign on the door.

> # Wanted:
> ### Delivery Driver
> ### Inquire Within

3   Right after he graduated, Joseph became Mr. Fellini, the "Pie Man." His work day started at 5 A.M. The bakers had already been at work for hours, putting together apple, cherry, peach, chocolate custard, banana cream, and all kinds of other pies. When Joseph arrived, the pies were in boxes and lined up on trays, ready for him to put into his truck. Joseph had always loved the smell of all those fresh pies, mingled and warm in the back of his truck. He never tired of that smell, even after 53 years on the job.

4   When Joseph was out in his truck, he felt important. The people who worked at the restaurants where he delivered the pies were always glad to see him. Out in traffic, people would sometimes make way for the Pie Man. They knew he had special cargo that needed to be delivered safe and fresh.

5   As Joseph strolled along Central Park West, he saw a pie truck. The young man at the wheel was beeping his horn impatiently. *Ah,* thought Joseph, *slow down. You still have 52 years to go.*

Vocabulary Skills

In each row below, circle the three words that belong together.

1. busy   street   avenue   road

2. job   college   work   career

3. bread   cake   delivery   pie

4. café   restaurant   diner   traffic

A **contraction** is one word that stands for two words. An apostrophe (') shows that one or more letters have been taken out. Write a contraction from the story for each pair of words below.

5. do not _____
   <small>Par. 1</small>

6. did not _____
   <small>Par. 2</small>

Replace the underlined words with a contraction. Write the contraction in the blank.

7. Mrs. Fellini thought <u>she would</u>
   _____ bake a pie.

8. The park <u>is not</u> _____ very busy in the morning.

9. I am glad <u>it is</u> _____ a sunny day.

Reading Skills

Write the best word to complete each sentence below.

1. Mr. Fellini read the _____ on the bakery door.
   (sled, sign, shore)

2. The _____ of pies must have been heavy.
   (trays, trains, tears)

3. Can you imagine the smells of all those pies _____ together?
   (muffled, mattered, mingled)

4. People seemed to respect the Pie Man's _____.
   (cargo, candle, credit)

5. Would you describe young Joseph as serious or dreamy? Write why.

   _____

   _____

   _____

6. How did Joseph feel about his job?

   _____

   _____

7. Do you think Joseph was a good worker? Explain.

   _____

   _____

   _____

Once a Pie Man, Always a Pie Man

What does Mr. Fellini do now that he doesn't deliver pies?

1   *Which way shall I go today?* Joseph thought to himself as the signs pointed this way and that. *I think Turtle Pond needs a visitor,* he decided. He followed the path to the right, toward the middle of Central Park. Around a curve, he had to step off the sidewalk as a line of mothers and baby strollers marched by. They didn't walk, they marched. Joseph had heard it called *power walking. I suppose it's good for them,* he thought, shaking his head. But he also thought their marching didn't allow them to notice the birds or the flowers.

2   At Turtle Pond, two young children had spied a turtle. It must have been their first one, judging by their excitement. Joseph smiled as he watched. He could remember being that excited about turtles when he was young.

3   From Turtle Pond, it was an easy walk to the art museum. Joseph sat down on a bench in the sun. He liked to watch all the different kinds of people go to the art museum. In a way, he thought the people were just like the pieces of art. Each one looked different and had a different reason for being there.

4   When he had soaked up enough sun, Joseph wandered toward Cedar Hill, then out to Fifth Avenue. A quick check of his watch told him he was right on time.

5   A pie truck pulled up.

6   "What'll it be today, Mr. Fellini?" said the young driver.

7   Joseph thought for a moment. "I think today is a peach day, Mr. Tarentino."

8   "Peach it is, Mr. Fellini," and the young man swung out of his seat and disappeared into the back of his truck. Behind the truck, cars waited, the drivers oddly patient. They knew the Pie Man had important business.

Vocabulary Skills

Check the meaning that fits the underlined word in each sentence.

1. Mr. Fellini had to <u>step</u> off the sidewalk.

_____ a short movement of the foot or feet

_____ a raised surface, usually in a series

2. Did you <u>notice</u> the turtles?

_____ see, observe

_____ a sign or poster

3. Mr. Fellini was sure to <u>check</u> his watch.

_____ an official paper that serves as money

_____ to look at quickly

Form the plural of each word below by adding **s**.

4. stroller _____

5. kind _____

6. piece _____

Form the plural of each word below by adding **es**.

7. bench _____

8. peach _____

9. bush _____

Reading Skills

1. As you began to read about Mr. Fellini's walk in the park, what did you think was going to happen?

_____

_____

_____

2. Predict what Mr. Fellini will do next.

_____

_____

_____

_____

3. Which of these does Mr. Fellini see on his walk?

_____ a work of art

_____ children and turtles

_____ mothers and baby strollers

_____ a nest of young birds

New York City's Gem

Find out what there is to see and do in Central Park.

1 It has been called "a wonder" and "an oasis." People go there to exercise or to relax. It is included on almost every tour of New York City because of its beauty. It is neither a historic building nor a skyscraper. It is Central Park.

2 Lying in the heart of Manhattan, Central Park is still the green space that its founders hoped it would be. As the city's population grew rapidly in the early 1800s, a few wise men saw the need to set aside some space that would give residents a break from the crowded city's hurry and noise.

3 The park's plan, developed in 1858, was a daring one. The chosen land was rocky, swampy, and muddy. For these reasons, the area was completely transformed in a project that took 20 years. Top soil from New Jersey came in horse-drawn carts. Lakes were dug. Boulders were blasted out, then carted away. Four million trees, shrubs, and plants were carted in and planted.

4 Though its appearance has changed during the last 150 years, Central Park continues to be an important place for tourists and New Yorkers alike.

Central Park by the Numbers	
25,000,000	Number of visitors to Central Park each year
26,000	Number of trees growing in Central Park
8,968	Number of benches in Central Park
843	Total acres of Central Park
275	Different types of birds found in Central Park
250	Number of acres of lawn in Central Park
150	Number of acres covered by water in Central Park
136	Number of wooded acres in Central Park
58	Total miles of walking paths in Central Park
6	Distance, in miles, around outside edge of Central Park

Vocabulary Skills

Words whose meanings are opposite are called **antonyms**. Match each word in the first list with its antonym in the second list. Write the letter in the blank.

1. _____ grow   **a.** shrink

2. _____ city   **b.** tight

3. _____ crowded   **c.** country

4. _____ loose   **d.** empty

Listen to the beginning sound of *central*. Circle the words below that have the same sound as the **c** in *central*. (The sound may be at the beginning, middle, or end of the word.)

5. cent   crack

6. fancy   color

7. credit   ceiling

8. pencil   pinch

Each sentence below contains a compound word. Find the word. Write the two small words that make up the compound word.

9. The view from the top of the skyscraper was great!

_____ _____

10. Mr. Fellini saw a goldfinch in a bush near the museum.

_____ _____

Reading Skills

1. The article contains a feature box titled "Central Park by the Numbers." What kind of information is in the box?

_____

_____

_____

2. Why do you think this information was shown in a separate list instead of in the text?

_____

_____

_____

3. When was Central Park planned?

_____

4. The park was a daring project because _____

_____

_____.

5. If you walked on all of the walking paths in the park, you would walk

_____.

6. Which is greater, the number of trees or the number of benches?

_____

Soccer Blues

Why is Perry so unhappy about soccer practice?

1   "Okay, everybody, come over here and listen up!" Coach's voice carried across the soccer field. Kids of all sizes and shapes stopped what they were doing and walked or trotted toward the coach. When the several dozen boys and girls were in a ring around him, the coach continued. "I want all of you to practice dribbling on your own for at least half an hour a day outside of practice. Okay?"

2   "Okay, Coach!" yelled the circle. Everyone smiled. Coach always liked answers to his questions.

3   Satisfied with the response, Coach went on. "Most of the passing we do in games is when we're only 10, maybe 20, yards apart. We need to be able to deliver the ball within that range *every time we pass*," Coach explained. "Now, we're going to do a one-on-one passing exercise. One partner over here, the other over there," he said, pointing to one touch line and another invisible line about half-way across the field. "What I want you to do is...."

4   Around the circle, heads nodded as eager players listened to Coach. One head, though, wasn't nodding; it was bobbing. Perry was so tired and hungry that his knees felt shaky. He was sure he had dribbled his soccer ball a hundred miles already this afternoon. He felt as if one more passing exercise would pretty much finish him off. Somehow, he stumbled through. He was pretty sure he did not impress Coach, though, when one of his passes went wildly across the field.

5   At the end of practice, Perry flopped into the back seat of the car and buckled his seatbelt. He didn't even wait for his mom's usual question.

6   "Practice was awful," said Perry without even opening his eyes. "I don't ever want to go back."

Vocabulary Skills

Write the words from the story that have these meanings.

1. jogged

   _____
   Par. 1

2. do something repeatedly

   _____
   Par. 1

3. hand over; transfer

   _____
   Par. 3

4. moved the head up and down

   _____
   Par. 4

5. tripped

   _____
   Par. 4

When a word has two consonants between two vowels, the syllables are usually divided between the two consonants. For example, *soccer* is divided like this: *soc / cer*.

For each word below, draw a line to divide the word into syllables.

6. c a r r y

7. a f t e r

8. p r e t t y

9. p r a c t i c e

Reading Skills

1. In most stories, a character has a problem. What is Perry's problem?

   _____

   _____

2. What information in the story helped you answer question 1?

   _____

   _____

   _____

3. **Dialogue** is what the characters in a story say. What did you learn about Perry from his dialogue?

   _____

   _____

4. Find a line of the coach's dialogue. What does it tell you about the coach?

   Dialogue: _____

   _____

   What it tells: _____

   _____

5. Coach thinks that a passing exercise is important because

   _____

   _____.

Mom to the Rescue

Have you ever solved a mystery?

1   Mrs. Rothman was speechless. The only thing Perry had talked about all winter was soccer. Now, Perry had said he wanted to quit soccer. Not knowing whether to laugh or cry, she drove home and fixed dinner.

2   After dinner, Mrs. Rothman tried to get to the bottom of the problem.

3   "Do you think Coach is too tough?"

4   "No."

5   "Are you having trouble with one of the other kids?"

6   "No."

7   "Did you get hurt?"

8   "No."

9   "Do you feel as if you're not good enough? If that's the case, you should talk to Coach...."

10   "Well, that's sort of it. I just felt so weak during practice. My knees were shaky. I could hardly lift my feet." Perry shook his head. "I just don't have what it takes. A soccer player has to run and run and not even get winded."

11   *Hmm,* thought Mrs. Rothman. *Weak? Shaky knees?* She softened her questioning a little. "Did you have a good lunch today?"

12   Perry thought for a second. "Um, yes, I guess so. Oh, except that there was a fire drill, and I didn't get to finish."

13   *Aha, that's it! A boy can't make it through school and soccer practice without the proper fuel.*

14   "I'll tell you what, Perry," said Mrs. Rothman, patting his knee. "Why don't you try it for one more day. I'll meet you after school with a power snack, and we'll see if that helps." Perry agreed, but he wondered what a power snack was and how it could possibly help.

Vocabulary Skills

Write the words from the story that have these meanings.

1. unable to say anything

_____
Par. 1

2. unsteady; wobbly

_____
Par. 10

3. be done

_____
Par. 12

To show that something happened in the past, add **ed** to a base word. Some words, however, do not follow normal spelling patterns. Read each sentence. Write the correct word in the blank.

ran	drove	shook

4. Today, I shake my head. Last week, I _____ my head.

5. Today, I run. Yesterday, I _____.

6. Today, you drive. Yesterday, you _____.

Complete each sentence below by writing the correct word in the blank.

7. This is the last _____ of practice before school starts. (weak, week)

8. I thought we agreed to _____ at 10 o'clock. (meat, meet)

Reading Skills

1. Mrs. Rothman is speechless because _____

_____.

2. Check two words that tell how Perry probably felt.

_____ disappointed

_____ proud

_____ eager

_____ frightened

3. Perry says he wants to quit soccer because _____

_____.

4. Have you ever tried to do something that was hard, or that you had to work at? What was it?

_____

_____

Did you get discouraged? Did you quit?

_____

_____

5. Do you think Perry's decision is reasonable, or do you think he is giving up too easily? Explain.

_____

_____

_____

Power Snack

Have you ever had a power snack?

Energy Bars

1 c. brown sugar	1 c. peanuts (optional)
1 c. vegetable oil	1 c. coconut (optional)
2 eggs	$1\frac{1}{2}$ tsp. ground cinnamon
2 C. oats	$1\frac{1}{2}$ tsp. ground cloves
$1\frac{1}{2}$ c. flour	1 tsp. baking soda
1 c. raisins	$\frac{1}{4}$ tsp. salt

Heat oven to 350° F. Grease 11" x 17" pan. Mix brown sugar, oil, and eggs until smooth. Stir in remaining ingredients. Spread mixture into pan, pressing with fingers until even. Bake until center is set, but not firm, 16–22 minutes. Remove from oven and cool for 15 minutes. Drizzle honey glaze* over bars. Let cool completely. Cut into squares. Store covered for two weeks. Or, wrap tightly and freeze for up to six months.

*Directions for honey glaze: Place $\frac{1}{4}$c. honey and 2 T. butter or margarine in a sauce pan. Heat and stir until well blended and heated through. Drizzle over bars.

(Note: Always ask a grown-up for help in the kitchen.)

Vocabulary Skills

Circle the word that correctly completes each sentence. Write the word in the blank.

1. When you use _____ sugar, pack it into the measuring cup.

   down   brown   crowd

2. Does it ask for stick cinnamon or _____ cinnamon?

   sound   cloud   ground

3. I think the best part is the plump, juicy _____.

   chain   raisins   plain

Recipes often use short forms of words called **abbreviations**. Match the common recipe words in the box with their abbreviations.

cup	teaspoon
Fahrenheit	tablespoon

4. T. _____

5. c. _____

6. F _____

7. tsp. _____

Recipes use many action words. Choose one of the action words in the box and write, in your own words, what you would do. Look back at the recipe for ideas.

stir	spread
mix	drizzle

Action word: _____

_____

_____

Reading Skills

Write these steps in the correct order. (Not all of the recipe's steps are here.)

- spread mixture into pan
- drizzle glaze
- grease the pan
- mix sugar, oil, and eggs
- remove from oven and cool

1. _____

2. _____

3. _____

4. _____

5. _____

6. How long do the directions say to bake the bars?

   _____

7. The directions say to "drizzle honey glaze over bars." How did you know what honey glaze was?

   _____

   _____

And It's Out of the Park!

What happens at the soccer game?

1   "Okay, everybody listen up!" coach said. It took only a moment for the team to gather. It was the first game of the season. Perry could tell that everyone was nervous and excited, just like he was.

2   "This is where all those drills pay off. You guys have dribbled to the moon and back since we started practice. You've done a good job. Now let's remember everything we learned and play a good game. Okay?"

3   "Okay!" the team yelled, and Coach smiled. He liked their spirit.

4   "All right! Let's go, Bobcats!" Perry and his teammates roared onto the field and took their positions.

5   It seemed as if Coach's hopes were coming true. The midfielders stayed in position. The center backs defended the goal well. Coach even heard some of the other team's parents admiring how his team handled the ball.

6   Neither team scored in the first half. During the second half, there was a great play that almost put a goal on the scoreboard in the final seconds.

7   There was a terrific jumble around the ball. Perry and another player were down, leaving two other players battling it out. Perry rolled out of the way and scrambled to his feet. Just then, the ball somehow broke free and came his way. Without hesitating for a moment, he reeled back and kicked.

8   *Now that was a solid kick*, Perry thought to himself. Time seemed to stop as everyone on the field watched the arch of the ball's flight. It was beautiful. When the ball disappeared from sight, someone in the crowd yelled, "It's a home run!" The crowd and the players exploded in laughter. In the midst of all the end-of-game confusion, Perry's only thought was, *Wow, those power snacks really work.*

Vocabulary Skills

Check the meaning that fits the underlined word in each sentence.

1. Perry thought <u>drills</u> were the worst part of practice.

   _____ repeated practice

   _____ tools used to make holes

2. The first game of the <u>season</u> was the most exciting one.

   _____ to add flavor

   _____ a period of time

3. There was nothing like the feel of a good, <u>solid</u> kick of the ball.

   _____ strong or sturdy

   _____ not liquid

4. Neither team had made a <u>goal</u>.

   _____ a score in a game or sport

   _____ something you try to reach

Add **ed** to these words to show that the actions happened in the past.

5. learn _____

6. yell _____

7. roar _____

Add **d** to some words that end in silent **e** to show that these actions happened in the past.

8. dribble _____

9. like _____

10. handle _____

Reading Skills

1. When you read the story's title, did you guess at the end of the story? Was your guess close to correct? Explain.

   _____

   _____

   _____

   _____

2. Circle the word that best describes the coach's words before the game.

   angry   encouraging

3. Have you ever been in a sporting event or a performance that didn't turn out the way you expected? Did something funny or weird happen? Write about it.

   _____

   _____

   _____

   _____

History of Soccer

Read to see how soccer had its start.

Earliest Record

1 The earliest written evidence of a soccer-like game comes from China. During the second and third centuries B.C., Chinese soldiers took part in an activity that involved kicking a ball into a small net. Historians think the game was a skill-building exercise for the soldiers.

Years of Development

2 In ancient Greece and Rome, teams of up to 27 players played a soccer-type game. In Britain hundreds of years later, during the thirteenth century A.D., whole villages played against each other. With hundreds of people playing, these games were both long and rough. Kicking, punching, and biting were common and allowed.

3 In 1331, the English King Edward III passed a law in an attempt to put a stop to the popular but violent game. The king of Scotland spoke against the game a hundred years later. Queen Elizabeth I, during the late 1500s, passed a law that called for a week of jail for anyone caught playing "football," or soccer, as we call it. But the game could not be stopped.

The Modern Game Emerges

4 Two hundred and fifty years later, people in Britain were still playing a game we would recognize as soccer. A well-known English college, Eton, developed a set of rules in 1815. A number of other colleges soon agreed to use the same rules, and those schools played against each other. Finally, 50 years later, a formal association formed to oversee the playing of the game and its rules. In 1869, a rule against handling the ball with the hands transformed the game into the sport of soccer that is wildly popular all around the world.

Vocabulary Skills

Write the words from the article that have these meanings.

1. something that gives proof

_____
Par. 1

2. physical activity to become stronger or more skilled

_____
Par. 1

3. done with force or violence

_____
Par. 2

4. to watch over or direct

_____
Par. 4

Circle the correct letters to complete each word. Write the letters in the blank.

5. Soccer dates to the second or th_____d century B.C.

ir   er   or

6. Can you imagine whole villages playing against each oth_____?

ar   ir   er

Reading Skills

1. This article is mostly about

_____ how soccer was named.

_____ the rules of soccer.

_____ soccer's history.

2. Historians think that soccer might have started out as a _____

_____.

3. Why did King Edward III pass a law against soccer?

_____

_____

4. What punishment did Queen Elizabeth have for soccer players?

_____

_____

5. What important rule change made the game into what we know as soccer? When did it happen?

_____

_____

Study Skills

1. If you wanted to find out about the beginnings of soccer, under which heading should you look?

_____

2. Under which heading would you find information about soccer during the last century or so?

_____

Why Soccer?

Why do you think soccer is so popular?

1   On what topic do more than 13 million American kids agree? Soccer! The Soccer Industry Council of America reported in 1999 that all those kids were playing organized soccer. Add adults into the mix, and you come up with more than 18 million Americans playing soccer. What makes soccer so popular?

2   First, I think, there's the international appeal. Americans see that people in many other countries in the world are wildly excited about soccer. The excitement must be catching.

3   Second, soccer takes less equipment than some other sports, especially football. For that reason, it's not very costly for a kid to join a soccer team.

4   Third, parents view soccer as a safer sport than some other sports. Though accidents may occur, body contact isn't supposed to be part of the game. Therefore, fewer injuries occur.

5   Fourth, soccer appeals to both boys and girls. Though soccer was at first only a male sport (just like all other sports), soccer has caught on with girls. This is good for the sport, I think. Interest in the sport extends to whole families, so there are more players, more fans, more coaches, and so on.

6   Finally, I think there is the running factor. Running up and down a field chasing a ball is such a healthy, all-American thing to do. Kids love it, and few parents can object to it.

Vocabulary Skills

In each row below, circle the three words or phrases that belong together.

1. T-shirt   soccer   football   hockey

2. helmet   pads   field   shin guards

3. running   kicking   passing   eating

A **contraction** is one word that stands for two words. Write a contraction from the story for each pair of words below.

4. there is _____
   Par. 2

5. it is _____
   Par. 3

6. is not _____
   Par. 4

When adding **ing** to a base word that ends in a silent **e**, drop the **e**, then add the ending. So, *take* becomes *taking*. Add **ing** to each word. Write the new word on the line.

7. organize _____

8. chase _____

9. come _____

10. score _____

Reading Skills

1. The person who wrote this article is the **author**. The author probably wrote this article to

   _____ make you laugh.

   _____ give information.

   _____ persuade you to do something.

The author states some facts in the article. She also gives her opinion. Write **F** next to each sentence that is a fact. Write **O** next to each sentence that gives an opinion.

2. _____ Add adults into the mix, and you come up with more than 18 million Americans playing soccer.

3. _____ First, I think, there's the international appeal.

4. _____ Though accidents may occur, body contact isn't supposed to be part of the game.

5. _____ And finally, I think there is the running factor.

6. Look back at the sentences you marked as opinions. What do you notice about them?

   _____

   _____

A Teacher's Journal

Do you think the girls will be able to work together?

April 14

1   When my students work together on projects, everything usually works out. I had my doubts today, though, when I put Sharla, Tess, and Lee together to make a volcano. At one point, I knew something was going to blow up, and it wasn't the volcano!

2   I knew the girls weren't good friends, but I encourage my students to learn to work with all of their classmates. I could tell they felt a little shy when they sat down for their first planning meeting. Students in other groups had questions, so I didn't notice the girls for quite a few minutes. When I looked back in their direction, one looked mad, one looked sad, and one was nearly in tears. Good grief!

3   As I approached, they all started talking at once. Tess didn't want to have to touch "that icky paste" to build the volcano. Sharla had some design ideas that she couldn't get across to the other two. Lee thought they should just stop talking and get to work.

4   I calmed the girls down and suggested that they make a list of things on which they agreed. They agreed they were making a volcano out of flour, salt, and water, and that's all. They couldn't agree on the size, on a base for the volcano, or on who should get to mix the paste. Each girl had her own ideas and would not budge for the sake of working together or moving ahead.

5   By this time, the work session was over and it was time for lunch. So the girls made very little progress, and I was wondering if I had made a big mistake. Maybe this was one group of students who just couldn't work together.

Vocabulary Skills

Write the words from the story that have these meanings.

1. tasks that require time and effort

   _____
   Par. 1

2. uncertainties; requests for information

   _____
   Par. 2

3. thoughts; plans for how something might be done

   _____
   Par. 3

4. movement forward or onward

   _____
   Par. 5

Circle the pair of synonyms in each row.

5. encourage   rise   lengthen   support

6. angry   approach   doubt   mad

7. question   mix   stir   agree

8. notice   together   shy   bashful

Reading Skills

1. Do you think Sharla, Tess, and Lee will be able to work together? Write why or why not.

   _____

   _____

   _____

2. Think of times when you worked with classmates on projects. Was it hard or easy? Explain.

   _____

   _____

   _____

3. Would you say that you are more like Sharla—full of ideas, or more like Lee—eager to stop talking and get to work? Write why.

   _____

   _____

   _____

4. Does the teacher who is writing the journal seem thoughtful or worn out? Write why you think so.

   _____

   _____

   _____

Study Skills

Number each list of words below in alphabetical order.

1. ____ blow   2. ____ questions

   ____ volcano   ____ groups

   ____ projects   ____ could

   ____ everything   ____ classmates

A Student's Journal

Read to see how the girls are moving ahead with their volcano.

April 16

1 Tess and Lee and I have to make a volcano together. Mrs. Holt put us in a group on Tuesday, and we had such a big argument! Tess was fussing about the paste and Lee didn't want to plan anything. She just wanted to jump in and start working. It was awful. We didn't get anything done. Yesterday, Mrs. Holt made us stay in during recess so we could finish planning our volcano. Missing recess was so unfair!

2 Anyway, we finally said we would make the volcano about a foot high, and we'd add a little village around the base. That way, Tess can make the little village since she refuses to touch the volcano paste. (I think Mrs. Holt should make her.)

3 Today, Lee and I mixed up the paste. It was really goopy but kind of fun. We set up a plastic water bottle and some wadded-up aluminum foil as a base for the volcano. Then, we started plopping paste on. Tess just watched (no fair).

4 I was making my side all nice and smooth. I told Lee she should smooth out her side, too. She said, "No, Sharla, it should look lumpy, like a real mountain," just as if she were the boss. I said it would just look messy and that we should make it smooth. Well, the whole thing went downhill from there. Our paste started to dry out, and we didn't have time to finish. I suppose that means we'll have to miss recess again tomorrow, and it's all Lee's fault.

Vocabulary Skills

Write the words from the story that have these meanings.

1. a sticky substance

   _____
   Par. 1

2. putting or placing somewhat carelessly

   _____
   Par. 3

A **compound word** is made by combining two smaller words. Find the compound word in each sentence. Write the two small words that make up the compound.

3. Tess was fussing about the paste and Lee didn't want to plan anything.

   _____   _____

4. Well, the whole thing went downhill from there.

   _____   _____

The prefix **un-** means "not." So, *unable* means "not able."

Read the words below. Write the correct word next to its meaning.

unhappy   unfair   uncertain

5. not certain _____

6. not happy _____

7. not fair _____

Reading Skills

This story is written in the form of a journal entry. The person who is writing uses *I* to refer to herself. She is the **narrator**, or the person telling the story.

1. Find a sentence that tells you that the narrator actually took part in the action of the story. Write the sentence here.

   _____

   _____

2. The narrator, Sharla, disagreed with Lee about _____

   _____.

3. Sharla was upset because

   _____

   _____.

Each of the following sentences contains a pronoun. Write which word the pronoun stands for.

4. Lee didn't want to plan anything, she just wanted to jump in.

   She stands for _____.

5. Tess can make the little village since she refuses to touch the volcano paste.

   She stands for _____.

The End of a Volcano Tale

What did the girls learn from their project?

1 Sharla, Tess, and Lee stood proudly behind their model volcano. Tess straightened a tiny building in the village at the base of the mountain.

2 Mrs. Holt quieted the class. "Girls, you may begin."

3 Lee felt something wiggly in her stomach. She was supposed to go first.

4 "This is our volcano," she said. *Oh, that was stupid*, thought Lee, trying not to roll her eyes. *They can probably figure that out.* "We made it this shape because that's how a lot of volcanoes are shaped."

5 Next, Sharla told about what happens when a volcano erupts. After that, Tess told about a famous volcano and the town nearby that got covered up with ash and mud.

6 When it looked as if they were done, Mrs. Holt had a question. "Can you tell about the steps you went through to complete your project, girls?"

7 The girls looked at each other. They hadn't expected this. Sharla felt her face turn red, but she spoke up.

8 "Well, at first we didn't agree about what we wanted and how we wanted to do it." Sharla shrugged. "It took us a while to make a plan and get it done."

9 Tess went on. "We figured out that everybody had a job to do."

10 "And everybody has good ideas, even if they're not what you expect," added Lee.

11 Mrs. Holt looked pleased. *It only took one volcano and two explosions to figure out how to work together*, she thought. *Not bad.*

Vocabulary Skills

Write the words from the story that have these meanings.

1. feeling pleased and satisfied

   _____
   Par. 1

2. sends forth steam, lava, and ash

   _____
   Par. 5

3. to finish

   _____
   Par. 6

4. to think the same; to have the same ideas

   _____
   Par. 8

A word without an ending is a **base** word. Circle the base word in each of the words below.

5. trying   6. shaped

7. covered   8. girls

9. pleased

Complete each sentence, using apostrophes correctly to show ownership.

10. This volcano belongs to the girls. It is the _____ volcano.

11. The students had questions. The _____ questions were good ones.

12. The teachers went on vacation. The _____ vacations were well deserved.

Reading Skills

1. This story is mostly about

   _____ becoming best friends after working together.

   _____ what the girls learned from their project.

   _____ how a teacher helped the girls get along.

2. How do the girls feel about their volcano project?

   _____

3. When it is Lee's turn to speak, she feels

   _____ nervous.

   _____ happy.

   _____ cross.

4. Why did Sharla's face turn red when Mrs. Holt asked about how they completed their project?

   _____

   _____

5. What experiences have you had working with other people? Were there times when you didn't agree or get along? Write about it.

   _____

   _____

   _____

   _____

   _____

Volcanoes

Read to find out why volcanoes erupt.

[1] The surface of Earth is not a solid place. There are many holes, some of which allow magma to reach the earth's surface from deep inside.

[2] Magma comes from deep inside Earth where it's hot. It's so hot that rocks melt. Magma is **molten**, or melted, rock. Because of the heat, there is also pressure. When things such as air, gases, or molten rock get hot, they **expand**, or get bigger. That means they need space. Weak parts of Earth's crust get pushed aside, or opened up. The magma follows the easiest path, usually along **fissures**, or cracks, toward the surface.

[3] When it does reach the surface, magma is called *lava*. If there is a great deal of pressure behind the magma, it explodes through the crust's surface, sending dust, ash, lava, and rocks high into the air. When there is only a little pressure, the magma may simply bubble up and form a lava flow that spreads across the land.

[4] A volcano may be **active**, or experience eruptions, on a fairly regular basis. Or it may lie **dormant**, or inactive, for hundreds of years. Scientists, called *volcanologists*, are always ready to learn more because each volcano is unique and may teach them something new about the inner workings of Earth.

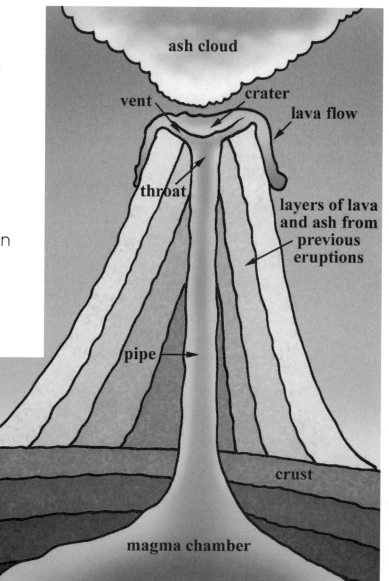

Vocabulary Skills

Write the words from the article that have these meanings.

1. not strong

_____
Par. 2

2. being the only one of its kind

_____
Par. 4

Listen to the sound of the **g** in *magma*. Circle the words below that have the same sound as the **g** in *magma*. (The sound may be at the beginning, middle, or end of the word.)

3. change   flag

4. garden   page

5. began   danger

6. gentle   goose

The words below are broken into syllables. Sound out each syllable. Then, write the word and say it to yourself as you write.

7. vol/ca/nol/o/gist _____

8. e/rup/tions _____

Reading Skills

In nonfiction writing, the author sometimes calls attention to words that the reader may not know. Those words appear in **bold** type. The author usually gives the meaning of the bold word in the same sentence.

Below are the bold words from the article. Write the meaning of each word.

1. molten _____

2. expand _____

3. fissures _____

4. active _____

5. dormant _____

Write **F** next to each sentence that is a fact. Write **O** next to each sentence that is an opinion.

6. _____ Volcanic eruptions are one of the most striking natural events.

7. _____ A volcanic eruption is more frightening than a hurricane.

8. _____ Volcanoes are located in many places in the world.

Study Skills

1. What does the illustration show?

_____

2. Trace with your finger the path that magma would take from under Earth's crust to the surface. Describe the path in your own words.

_____

_____

_____

And the Next Unit Is...

What will Miss Eller's class learn about next?

1 The classroom hummed with the usual Monday morning activity. Students emptied their backpacks, signed in, did their morning math problems, and chattered about the weekend.

2 Miss Eller called the students to Morning Meeting and watched while they got settled. Finally, she said, "Happy Monday morning, everyone." A chorus of greetings came back.

3 "Today is a decision-making day," Miss Eller announced. A few eyebrows went up. "Today, we're ready to start a new unit." Miss Eller made sure everyone was really tuned in. "Our new unit is the natural world," said Miss Eller, and she wrote the words on the board. A hand went up.

4 "Where does the deciding come in?" Zach asked.

5 "Ah, I'm glad you asked," smiled Miss Eller. She circled her arms wide. "The natural world includes everything around us, and everything around other people, all over the world. That's too much for us to learn about, so we need to narrow our topic down quite a bit."

6 Kayla raised her hand. "Does that mean we have to pick one place in the world to learn about? I pick Alaska."

7 "That's the idea, Kayla, but even Alaska is a very big topic," answered Miss Eller. "We would have to narrow that down even further. Yes, Zach?"

8 "Would a grasshopper's knees be narrow enough?" Everyone giggled.

9 "Well, that might be a little too narrow, but grasshoppers would be an excellent topic. I want all of you to think about one thing in the natural world that you want to learn about. We'll talk about this again after lunch. Okay?" Everyone nodded.

10 "Now, whose turn is it to do the weather chart?" As Miss Eller started the daily routine, twenty-two busy brains were thinking up ideas.

Vocabulary Skills

In each group below, circle the three words that belong together.

1. math science backpack reading

2. weekend weather day month

3. lunch eyebrow knee hand

4. afternoon morning evening activity

Circle the correct letters to complete each word. Write the letters in the blank.

5. The next unit is about the natural w_____ld.

    er   or   ir

6. The classroom is always busy in the m_____ning.

    ar   or   er

7. She made a c_____cle with her arms.

    or   er   ir

8. The weath_____ chart is the first part of the day.

    er   ur   ir

Reading Skills

Write the best word to complete each sentence below.

1. The students were especially _____ on Monday morning. (noisy, rosy, nosy)

2. Miss Eller wrote the topic on the _____. (body, break, board)

3. The teacher waved her _____ all around. (aims, aches, arms)

4. Zach was only _____ about the grasshopper's knees. (kind, kidding, kitten)

5. What do Miss Eller's students do as they begin their day? Find five details from the story and list them in order.

    _____

    _____

    _____

    _____

6. What do you think will happen after lunch, when the students meet to talk about their new unit?

    _____

    _____

    _____

So Many Ideas

Read to find out what everyone wants to study.

1   Miss Eller's students clattered in from lunch recess. Balls and jump ropes landed in the recess basket. A line formed at the water fountain as hot and thirsty children waited for their turn to cool down. Miss Eller's quiet presence at the meeting rug was a signal for everyone to settle down and join her.

2   Miss Eller began when all mouths stopped, and all eyes were on her. "Have all of you been thinking about the natural world and what you would like to learn about?" Heads nodded and some hands shot up. "Tara?"

3   "I want to study wild animals," Tara stated simply.

4   Miss Eller challenged her. "There are many, many wild animals. Did you have any particular ones in mind?"

5   Tara looked at the ceiling and thought for a moment. "Just the cute, fuzzy ones that live in the woods."

6   "Hmm, well, that narrows it down. Keith?"

7   Keith was sure of himself. "Snakes. Just the coolest ones."

8   "Okay," nodded Miss Eller. "Snakes are certainly part of the natural world, and you narrowed down the topic a bit already. Anyone else? Andy?"

9   "Trees are an important part of the natural world, right?" asked Andy.

10   "Yes," agreed Miss Eller.

11   "But there are too many kinds," continued Andy, "so I would narrow them down to redwood trees. They're special because they're so big."

12   "They certainly are," said Miss Eller. "Anyone else?"

13   Hand after hand went up. Everyone had a different idea. Miss Eller listened carefully and thought to herself, *How will we ever agree on what to study?*

Vocabulary Skills

Write the words from the story that have these meanings.

1. feeling a need to drink liquid

   _____
   Par. 1

2. plainly

   _____
   Par. 3

3. a very short period of time

   _____
   Par. 5

Match each word in the first list with its antonym in the second list. Write the letter in the blank.

4. _____ narrow   a. same

5. _____ wild   b. fuzzy

6. _____ different   c. wide

7. _____ bald   d. tame

Have you heard this saying?

I before *e*, except after *c*, or when rhyming with *hay*, as in *neighbor* and *weigh*.

The words in this box follow the rule.

| **believe** | **ceiling** | **sleigh** |

Use the words to complete the sentences.

8. The snow made a _____ ride possible.

9. You wouldn't _____ me even if I told you.

10. I stared at the crack in the

    _____.

Reading Skills

1. Which of the students' ideas do you like best? Write why.

   _____

   _____

2. Write **R** next to the sentences that tell about what Miss Eller's students could do for their study of the natural world. Write **M** next to the sentences that are about made-up things.

   _____ Isaac goes to the South Pole.

   _____ Tina collects seeds.

   _____ Justin sets up a bird feeder.

   _____ Megan climbs the Alps.

3. What does this sentence from the story tell you about Miss Eller?

   "Miss Eller's quiet presence at the meeting rug was a signal for everyone to settle down and join her."

   _____

   _____

4. Look for another sentence that tells you something about Miss Eller. What does it tell you?

   _____

   _____

Too Many Ideas!

How will the class ever decide what to study?

1   Miss Eller stared at the board. It looked like a maze. She didn't know where to begin.

2   "That's quite a pack of ideas," said a voice from over her shoulder. It was Mrs. Samm, the fourth-grade teacher.

3   "Oh, hello, Gina," smiled Miss Eller. "I want the students to help decide what to study, but now I have to narrow this down to something we can manage." Miss Eller shook her head.

4   "It's too bad they can't all follow their own ideas," Mrs. Samm said. "The students will be more eager to learn if they're working on topics that they're already interested in." Mrs. Samm turned to go. "Well, good luck. I hope you can sell your solution, whatever it is."

5   Miss Eller was so distracted she didn't even notice Mrs. Samm leave. *Sell my solution….that's it!* Miss Eller snapped her fingers and finished getting ready for the day.

6   Later, at Morning Meeting, Miss Eller started to sell her solution.

7   "Andy, how much do you want to study redwoods?" she asked.

8   Andy shrugged. "A lot, I guess."

9   Miss Eller turned to Tara. "What about you and your fuzzy animals?"

10   "Oh, they're so cute," said Tara, wrinkling up her nose. "They're my favorite things."

11   "Okay," said Miss Eller to the whole group, "you're going to have to convince us that your topic is the best one. Each of you is going to do some research on your own topic this week. Then, you'll give a "sales pitch" to the class and try to convince us to choose your topic to study." She scanned the faces all around her. *Are they buying it?* she wondered.

12   "Miss Eller?" asked Keith. "Can I give out plastic snakes to help convince people?"

13   *Sold.*

Vocabulary Skills

Write the words from the story that have these meanings.

1. to make less wide or broad

   _____
   Par. 3

2. hairy, furry

   _____
   Par. 9

Choose the word that correctly completes the sentence and write it in the blank.

3. Miss Eller hoped the _____ class would buy the idea. (hole, whole)

4. The students will not be _____ if they choose their own topics. (board, bored)

5. Miss Eller really wants the students to _____ their ideas. (cell, sell)

Reading Skills

1. This story is mostly about

   _____ solving a problem.

   _____ how to do research.

   _____ getting ready for school.

2. Why does Miss Eller let the students offer so many ideas?

   _____

   _____

3. Write in your own words what Miss Eller's solution is.

   _____

   _____

   _____

Study Skills

To find the meaning of a word, look in a dictionary. Some words have more than one meaning. Look at the words and their meanings below. Answer the questions.

solo   a performance or action done by one person

solution   1 the answer to a problem; 2 a mixture of two or more substances

solve   to find the solution to

1. Which word means "to find the solution to"?

   _____

2. What is a solo?

   _____

   _____

3. Which meaning of *solution* is used in this sentence?

   Letting the students decide was a perfect solution.

   _____

Forest Mammals

Do you know what a mammal is?

Common Characteristics

1 What does a moose have in common with a porcupine? How about a bear with a mouse? How can more than 4,000 different kinds of mammals have much of anything in common? In fact, mammals have four distinct characteristics.

1. Mammals have warm blood, which means they can maintain a steady body temperature.

2. Mammals have backbones.

3. Female mammals produce milk to feed their babies.

4. Mammals have fur or hair, though the amount of it varies widely.

North American Forest Dwellers

2 Forest mammals are alike in that they live in the same natural conditions, or **habitat**. Trees and the leafy undergrowth provide shelter and food for the many types of mammals that live in a North American forest.

3 **Insect eaters** Moles and shrews are just two types of **insectivores** that live on or under the forest floor. They find insects in the dirt or in rotting tree trunks or leaf matter.

4 **Gnawing animals** This large family of mammals, called **rodents**, includes beavers, squirrels, mice, and porcupines. Whether on the ground or in trees, these animals gnaw on nuts, seeds, and branches with their strong front teeth.

5 **Hare-like animals** Rabbits and hares make up this group. Leafy sprouts and sometimes the bark of young trees are the main diet of these animals.

6 **Meat eaters** In North America, the largest meat eaters, or **carnivores**, are bears and mountain lions. Wolves and coyotes are also members of this group. They eat smaller mammals such as rabbits, mice, and moles.

7 **Hoofed animals** In North America, moose and deer are the most common forest-dwelling hoofed animals. The forest provides both shelter and food for them.

Vocabulary Skills

Circle the word that correctly completes each sentence. Write the word in the blank.

1. A mouse may live in the forest, or it may live in your _____.

   house   hose   how

2. Insect eaters might dig in the ground for their _____.

   felt   fair   food

3. Rodents use their strong front teeth to _____ on hard nuts and branches.

   gnaw   blow   growl

4. The most famous rodents are probably _____ because of the dams they make.

   trees   beavers   secrets

When a word has one consonant between two vowels, the break between the syllables depends on the first vowel. If the vowel has a long sound, as in *beaver*, the consonant goes with the second syllable: *bea / ver*. If the vowel has a short sound, as in *body*, the consonant stays with the first syllable: *bod / y*. For each word below, draw a line to divide the word into syllables.

5. e a t e r s   6. m a n y

7. f e m a l e   8. s t e a d y

9. l e a f y

Reading Skills

1. What four common characteristics do mammals have?

   _____
   _____
   _____
   _____

In the article, the author showed some words in bold type. The meanings of those words are given as well. Find the meanings of the words and write them here.

2. habitat _____

   _____

3. insectivores _____

   _____

4. rodents _____

   _____

5. carnivores _____

   _____

Snakes: Love Them or Leave Them?

Why do you think snakes are not popular?

1 I think it is safe to say that most people really don't like snakes. It would be hard to find a person who is neutral, or simply doesn't care one way or the other. What I can't figure out is why something that doesn't even have any legs causes such alarm.

2 Snakes are reptiles, of course, not mammals. Do you think there is some ancient hatred between mammals and reptiles? Maybe their cold-bloodedness is what makes us dislike snakes. Or perhaps age-old stories about frightening creatures with scales cause us to turn away from our neighbors the snakes.

3 Snakes are quite useful, but that doesn't seem to matter. Snakes help control the rodent population. Without snakes, perhaps we would be overrun with mice. Most of us, however, would rather see a mouse than a snake.

4 The poison argument is a strong one. Some snakes are poisonous, and people all over the world do die from snake bites each year. However, the poisonous varieties are only a small percentage of the world's snakes. We can't say the whole batch is bad just because of a few rotten ones.

5 And what do we do with the people who really like snakes? They like snakes even more strongly than we dislike them. These people learn about them, seek them out, and observe them. Why? The only reason I can think of is that these people are truly generous and open-minded. They are able to put aside differences and welcome the snake as a fellow living being.

6 Whatever the reason for our like or dislike, snakes are a vital part of the circle of life. They would prefer to be left alone, and that is what we should do. If you're lucky, you might not run across more than a few of them in an entire lifetime. That would be fine with most of us.

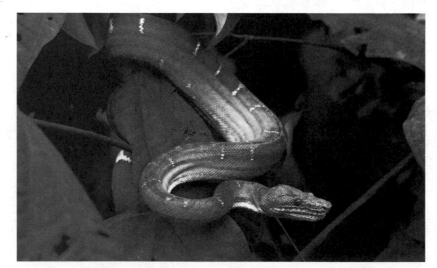

Vocabulary Skills

Some words are spelled the same, but have different meanings. For example, *yard* can mean "a unit of measure" or "land around a house." Check the meaning that fits the underlined word in each sentence.

1. Seeing a snake is no cause for <u>alarm</u>.

    _____ fear

    _____ a device for warning of danger

2. Do we dislike snakes because of their <u>scales</u>?

    _____ small overlapping plates on a fish or reptile's body

    _____ a device for measuring weight

3. Scientists may keep their research notes in a <u>safe</u>.

    _____ unlikely to cause or result in harm

    _____ a metal container for storing something valuable

Form the plural of each word below. Remember, if a word ends in **y**, change the **y** to **i** and add **es**. Write the word on the line.

4. snake _____

5. reptile _____

6. variety _____

7. mammal _____

8. story _____

9. creature _____

10. rodent _____

Reading Skills

The author of this article chose to share her own point of view. Find a sentence in which the author uses the word *I*. What idea is the author sharing in that sentence?

1. The sentence begins with

    _____.

    The author is saying _____

    _____.

2. Do you think the author likes snakes, dislikes snakes, or is neutral? Write a sentence from the article that supports your answer.

    _____

    _____

Write **F** next to each sentence that is a fact. Write **O** next to each sentence that is an opinion.

3. _____ People dislike snakes because they have no legs.

4. _____ Snakes control the rodent population.

5. _____ Not meeting many snakes is a good thing.

Redwood Giants

Read to learn about America's biggest trees.

1   From a seed that is smaller than a pea grows the tallest of trees. The coast redwood is the unchallenged giant of North America's trees.

What's special about redwoods?

2   Redwoods are special for a couple of reasons. The first is their size. Imagine standing next to a tree that is the height of a 20- or 30-story building. The second is their age. Redwoods commonly make it to 600 years or so. Some have been found that are more than 2,000 years old.

Where do redwoods grow?

3   To find a coast redwood, you'll have to go to Oregon or California. A strip of coastline about 450 miles long and up to 35 miles wide is home to the redwoods. Coast redwoods do not grow anywhere else in the world.

Why do redwoods grow there?

4   The coast of the Pacific Ocean provides a special environment for the redwoods. Cool, moist air comes off the ocean and keeps the trees moist all year. That is important because almost all of the area's rain falls between October and May. During the dry summer months, the trees depend on moisture from the thick fog that often hangs over the coast.

How do redwoods survive?

5   Redwoods have a couple of built-in protection systems. Most of a redwood's branches and leaves are high up on the tree. This keeps them safe from forest fires. Also, the bark of a mature redwood tree is as much as 12 inches thick. The thick covering protects the lower part of the tree from fire damage. Redwoods are safe from insect damage because the wood contains a bitter-tasting chemical called *tannin*.

What should I do?

6   If you ever get a chance, visit a redwood forest. Look among the tree trunks and imagine who might have camped there a thousand years ago. Look upward and just imagine how high the trees might grow if we preserve and protect them.

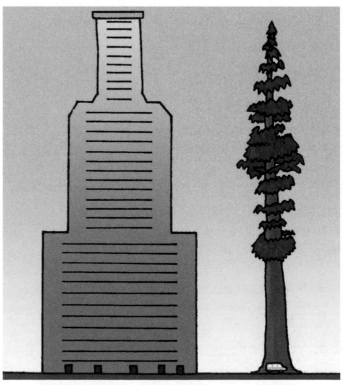

NAME _____

Vocabulary Skills

Write the words from the article that have these meanings.

1. huge; very tall

    _____
    Par. 1

2. regularly; normally

    _____
    Par. 2

3. damp; wet

    _____
    Par. 4

Units of measure are often abbreviated, or shortened. Write the correct abbreviation in each blank.

mi.	ft.	in.

4. The bark of a redwood is 12 _____ thick.

5. Redwoods grow within 35 _____ of the coast.

6. The tallest redwoods are more than 300 _____ high.

Reading Skills

1. To see a redwood tree, you have to go to _____.

2. Why do redwoods grow there?

    _____

    _____

3. What might happen if someone tried to grow a redwood tree in Kansas or Missouri, for example?

    _____

    _____

4. What do you think is most special about redwood trees? Write why.

    _____

    _____

    _____

Study Skills

1. Why do you think the author chose to use questions for the headings?

    _____

    _____

    _____

2. If you want to find out what conditions redwoods need to grow, under which heading would you look?

    _____

3. If you wonder what the big deal is about redwoods, under which heading should you look?

    _____

4. What three objects are shown in the diagram?

    _____

    _____

Spectrum Reading Grade 3

61

Problem Solved

What will Miss Eller decide the class should study?

1   So far, Miss Eller's idea had worked out. Her students had done some research on whatever they wanted to know about the natural world. They had all really enjoyed uncovering facts about snails or redwood trees or grasshoppers. And Keith's plastic snakes had been a big hit.

2   Now it all fell back to Miss Eller, though. She had to decide whose ideas to accept and whose to reject. She thought back on the students' reports and tried to sort them into groups. Furry things in this group, and crawling things in that group? No, that didn't really work.

3   Suddenly, her gaze shifted and she realized that the answer was right in front of her. A poster on the wall showed a lush woodland scene that included many different kinds of trees, forest creatures, birds, and, yes, even some snakes and crawly things. Miss Eller smiled. *A picture is worth a thousand words—or a thousand ideas,* she thought. She had the solution.

4   After lunch, the students gathered on the meeting rug. "What if I told you that we are going to have one topic, but that you are all going to be able to study what you want?"

5   "How can that be?" questioned Tara. "We all had different ideas."

6   Miss Eller shrugged. "It all depends on how you group things together. What if our topic is 'Redwood Forests'? What do you suppose lives in a redwood forest?"

7   Hands shot up left and right. Everything the students could think of fit into Miss Eller's topic: redwood trees, of course, cute and fuzzy mammals, snails, snakes—you name it.

8   Within a few weeks, the classroom had been transformed. A sign appeared outside the classroom door.

> ## Welcome to our
> # redwood forest.
> If something lives, grows, eats, breathes, or crawls in a redwood forest, we know all about it.
> ## Come on in.

NAME _____

Vocabulary Skills

Find the compound word in each sentence. In the blanks, write the two small words that make up the compound word.

1. Everything fit into Miss Eller's topic.

   _____   _____

2. Deer are a common woodland animal.

   _____   _____

3. Have you seen what they did to their classroom?

   _____   _____

4. I feel as if I'm outside, but I know I'm not.

   _____   _____

5. Scientists don't really know why redwood trees grow so tall.

   _____   _____

6. One student brought a grasshopper to school.

   _____   _____

The prefix **in-** means "not." So, *inactive* means "not active." Add **in** to the words below. Use the new words to complete the sentences.

| visible | dependent | decisive |

7. Miss Eller was pleased that the students were _____ enough to do their own research.

8. At first, Miss Eller was _____ about what topic they should study.

9. With all the forest decorations, the walls were nearly _____.

Reading Skills

Complete each sentence with the correct word.

| author | dialogue | narrator |

1. When characters speak, their words make up the story's _____.

2. The person who wrote the story is the _____.

3. Within the story, the person or character who tells the story is the _____.

4. In most stories, the main character has a problem. Miss Eller's problem is that _____ _____.

5. Look at the illustration. What did Miss Eller's students do during their study of redwood forests?

   _____
   _____
   _____
   _____

Spectrum Reading Grade 3

63

The Hamster from Room 144

What is unusual about this hamster?

1   I always knew Felix was special. He had been Mrs. Raymond's class pet for about 24 years. This summer, I was the lucky one who got to take him home. Felix, by the way, is a hamster.

2   As I said, I always knew he was special. Every school day when I checked on him, he would say, "Good morning, Tommy." That struck me as a little odd. When I saw him sitting in his cage counting on his claws during math class, I knew something was up for sure.

3   On the first day of summer, I took my allowance and my mom to the pet store. I bought some tunnels to add to Felix's cage. Felix loved his tunnels. By the end of the first week, Mom said, "Enough already," so I stopped adding tunnels. There were 376 feet of them.

4   One night, I couldn't fall asleep, so I went down to talk to Felix. He was running on his wheel. He apologized for not being able to chat, but he was trying to break a speed record. I watched for a while. I clocked him at 41 miles per hour.

5   The next night, Dad came down to watch. He had a brilliant idea. He hooked up a generator to Felix's wheel. Now, Felix makes electricity for us. We haven't had a bill from the electric company for two months.

6   Here's another reason I knew Felix was special. Back in Room 144, whenever it was time for music, I would see Felix tapping his little claws against the bars of the cage. He had excellent rhythm. During the summer, Felix took to writing his own songs. He even wrote one for Mrs. Raymond.

7   Now that summer is almost over, I'm kind of sad about having to take Felix back to Mrs. Raymond. Dad says he'll miss not having to pay any electric bills. Felix says not to worry. He has a plan for a new generator. Good old Felix.

Vocabulary Skills

Write the words from the tall tale that have these meanings.

1. saying numbers in order

   _____
   Par. 2

2. sum of money paid by parents to child

   _____
   Par. 3

3. long, narrow passages

   _____
   Par. 3

4. talk in a friendly, relaxed manner

   _____
   Par. 4

Words whose meanings are opposite are called **antonyms**. Match each word in the first list with its antonym in the second list. Write the letter in the blank.

5. _____ special   **a.** winter

6. _____ odd   **b.** ordinary

7. _____ summer   **c.** even

Reading Skills

In a tall tale, the author uses details that can't possibly be true to make the story funny. This is called **exaggeration**. Exaggeration is what makes a tall tale a tall tale.

1. Tommy, the narrator, tells us that the hamster has lived for 24 years.

That is an exaggeration. Find another exaggeration in the story.

_____

_____

2. Look at what you wrote for question 1. Why or how is it an exaggeration?

_____

_____

Study Skills

In some dictionaries, entry words are shown divided into syllables. For example, the entry for *hamster* would look like this: **ham • ster**. If you ever have to break a word at the end of a line of writing, do it between syllables.

Read each word. Then, write the number of syllables it has.

1. al • ways _____

2. sum • mer _____

3. fin • gers _____

4. checked _____

5. e • lec • tric _____

6. com • pa • ny _____

7. mu • sic _____

8. ex • cel • lent _____

Caring for a Pet Hamster

What does it take to care for a hamster?

1. You and your parents agree that you are ready for a pet. A dog is too big. Mom is allergic to cats. So a hamster is everyone's number one choice. What will it take to keep your new pet safe and happy?

2. Choose a hamster from a pet store that is clean and whose staff seems to know about the animals and is willing to answer your questions. If the hamsters are not used to being handled, you probably want to choose a younger one. You'll be able to tame and handle a younger one more easily than an older one.

3. Before you get your hamster, you should have its new home all set up. Hamsters need several pieces of equipment, but the only one that is somewhat expensive is the cage. Here are the items your hamster must have: a cage, bedding (wood shavings), nesting material (cotton), an exercise wheel, a water bottle, a food dish, and food.

4. Almost all of your hamster's life will be spent in the cage, and it needs room to move around. Buy the largest cage you can afford. A wire cage is best if you have a draft-free place for it. If the cage has to sit near a vent, window, or door, then a plastic or glass type with a screen top is better.

5. Make sure that your hamster has fresh water at all times. A general hamster mix from the pet store will make up most of your pet's diet. Beyond that, learn what other foods you can give as treats. Some examples are carrots, raisins, cheese, dog biscuits, and acorns. In general, do not feed your hamster sweets or prepared foods, such as crackers or chips.

6. With daily food and water, regular attention, and a weekly cage cleaning, your hamster should be a happy addition to your household for several years.

Vocabulary Skills

In each row below, circle the three words that belong together.

1. cat   dog   hamster   giraffe

2. exercise   tame   gentle   calm

3. draft   crate   barn   cage

4. feather   fur   hair   tail

Listen to the sound of the **c** in *cage*. Circle the words below that have the same sound as the **c** in *cage*. (The sound may be at the beginning, middle, or end of the word.)

5. clean   face

6. decide   because

7. cold   cent

8. allowance   become

Reading Skills

1. What do you know about taking care of a pet? How is taking care of a hamster the same or different from taking care of other kinds of pets?

   _____

   _____

   _____

2. In the wild, hamsters sleep during the day and gather food during the night. Pet hamsters tend to follow the same schedule. If someone is thinking of getting a hamster, why is this important information to know?

   _____

   _____

Study Skills

The author forgot to include headings in the article. Write where each heading should go.

1. **Equipment** should go before the _____ paragraph.

2. **Feeding Time** should go before the _____ paragraph.

3. **Choosing a Pet** should go before the _____ paragraph.

An **encyclopedia** contains facts about many different topics. Each book, or volume, includes topics that begin with certain letters of the alphabet. Look at the set of encyclopedias below. Then, write the number of the volume you could use to find the topics listed.

4. glass _____   5. Asia _____

6. exercise _____   7. marble _____

Skyway Sweeper

What does Frederick think about as he works?

1   *Swish, swush. Swish, swush.* Frederick had always thought the broom had two different sounds to it. *Swish* was the outward stroke; *swush* was the inward stroke. It was the only sound he heard all day, really. The padded plastorub floors of the skyways didn't make any noise. Most people wore shoes made of plastorub as well, so there was no chance of making a sound.

2   Noise had become a big issue about a century ago. There were so many people making so much noise that no one could stand it. People wore ear plugs. New illnesses were blamed on noise pollution. Governments passed laws against noise. Then, a team of scientists came up with plastorub. People put it everywhere, and the noise died down.

3   Between plastorub and the big building boom, things were pretty quiet now. The buildings were so big and so tall that people didn't even have to go outside. People lived, worked, and shopped all in the same building.

4   Not Frederick, though. Frederick was a sweeper. Each night he slept in a different sweeper's lodge as he made his rounds from skyway to skyway. *Swish, swush. Swish, swush.*

5   Frederick liked his job. He liked seeing how things changed from one year to the next. Buildings went up or came down. Skyways sprouted and branched off to new places. He always liked the view, no matter what it was.

6   Through all of his sweeping travels, though, Frederick had never set foot on the ground. He had seen it a few times, through a window, but he had never actually stepped on it. People said it was hard and unpleasant. He imagined taking off his plastorub shoes and walking barefoot, just to feel the solid planet underneath him. Frederick wondered what it was like to hear a footstep.

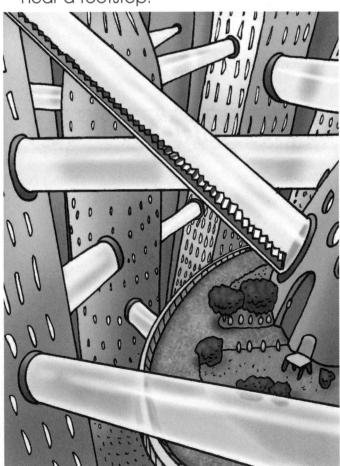

Vocabulary Skills

Complete each sentence below by adding the correct ending to the word given at the end of the sentence.

1. The broom _____ as Frederick swept the skyway. (swish)

2. Frederick liked that the view was always _____. (change)

3. By _____ special shoes, people made no noise when they walked. (wear)

4. Frederick had only _____ the ground. (imagine)

5. He had always _____ thinking about the ground. (like)

6. Frederick liked _____ in a different place each night. (sleep)

Add **'s** to a singular word or **'** to a plural word to show who owns something.

7. the lodge belongs to a sweeper

_____

8. the job belongs to the managers

_____

9. the building belongs to a family

_____

10. the brooms belong to sweepers

_____

Reading Skills

1. The story gives details about Frederick and the world in which he lives. Number these details in the order in which the story gives them.

_____ Noise had been a problem.

_____ Frederick liked his job.

_____ Frederick is a skyway sweeper.

_____ The skyway floors are padded.

_____ People stayed inside all the time.

_____ Frederick had never stepped on the ground.

2. As the story gives details, several sounds are mentioned. What are they?

_____

_____

Each of the following sentences contains a pronoun. Tell what word the pronoun stands for.

3. When Frederick pushed the broom, it made a swishing sound.

It stands for _____.

4. Frederick remembered the day he had seen the ground.

He stands for _____.

Rooftop Keeper

Read to find out what sirt is and how Frederick feels about it.

1   *Sssssssssssssssss.* The sirt sifted between Frederick's fingers. He was used to the feel and the sound of it, but he wondered...well, there was no use in wondering.

2   Real dirt had been used up long ago. There were so many people to feed, and there were so many buildings covering up the ground. The whole idea of farming had been reinvented. That's when sirt was invented. The scientists called it *sirt* to make people think of *soil* and *dirt*, but most people didn't know what was in it. Sirt did make things grow, though, and that's what counted.

3   When he wasn't sweeping skyways, Frederick was the Head Rooftop Keeper for Building Q4-S621-B88. It was his job to grow fresh fruits and vegetables and supply them to the families who lived down below. Frederick took pride in his crops. Nothing pleased him more than when someone commented on his shiny apples or his crunchy carrots.

4   *Sssssssss* went the sirt again as Frederick scooped and sifted, preparing the surface for some new seeds. He crinkled his nose as the faint chemical smell of the sirt reached him. He had read about people who, a long time ago, would kiss the dirt and talk to it. Frederick couldn't imagine kissing sirt. He couldn't imagine...well, he couldn't imagine a lot of things.

5   What did wet dirt feel like? Sirt didn't change, whether it was wet or dry. That was the chemicals, Frederick supposed. Did dirt run through your fingers just like sirt? *Ah, there's no use wondering,* he scolded himself. Frederick shook the sirt off his hands and took hold of his broom handle to begin the day's work. *Still, I wonder...*

Vocabulary Skills

Write the words from the story that have these meanings.

1. to use land for growing crops

   _____
   Par. 2

2. recently harvested

   _____
   Par. 3

3. to give or make available

   _____
   Par. 3

4. stated; gave an opinion

   _____
   Par. 3

Circle the word that is a synonym of the underlined word in each sentence.

5. Frederick wondered what sound real dirt made.

   clank   noise   rattle

6. Making people happy with his crops pleased Frederick.

   entertained   worried   delighted

7. Frederick could never get used to that faint chemical odor.

   thin   pale   weak

Circle the correct letters to complete each word. Write the letters in the blank.

8. All that Frederick could think about was d_____t.

   ur   er   ir

9. F_____ming had changed completely since the old, old days.

   er   ar   ur

10. Frederick smoothed the s_____face to prepare for planting seeds.

    ur   ar   er

Reading Skills

1. Write **R** next to the sentences that tell about something real. Write **M** next to the sentences that are about made-up things.

   _____ People do not know what dirt feels like.

   _____ The whole world is covered up with buildings.

   _____ People grow vegetables in gardens.

   _____ People stay indoors and never have to go outside.

In some stories, the problem is obvious. Maybe the character breaks an arm and has to learn how to write with the other hand, or something like that. In this story, the problem is not as obvious.

2. What problem does this character have?

   _____

   _____

   _____

Frederick's Secret

Read to see how Frederick's dream leads to Frederick's secret.

1   No sunlight reached the ground. Frederick hadn't stopped to think about that. Of course, it made sense, though. The buildings were so tall and so close together. But more than the lack of sunlight, it was the airlessness that Frederick noticed. It was so still and stale that Frederick almost had to work to breathe.

2   The idea had come about slowly. The *swish-swush* of his broom up in the skyways had become *sirt-dirt, sirt-dirt.* Frederick had grown up with sirt, the special chemical mix that was used in place of dirt in his rooftop garden. But to feel the ground and touch real dirt—that's what he thought about constantly, and that's what brought about his plan.

3   After many weeks of thinking and of finding courage, Frederick had made his way down to the surface. Now, he followed streets and paths, looking for a bare patch of ground. It took so long. He began to panic, thinking he would never find one. Then, two more left turns and Frederick's dream came true.

4   Frederick ran to the small bare patch of dirt, missed somehow by the builders years ago. Tears welled up in his eyes as he fell to his knees, touching the ground with his fingers, smelling it, even kissing it. Then, his shoes were off, and he was standing, bare-footed, wiggling his toes, stomping his feet, actually hearing the soft thud of his own footsteps. Frederick stood there, looking straight upward through his tears, until the sky began to darken. Then, he filled his shoes with dirt and made his way back to his rooftop garden.

5   Six months later, Frederick received an award from the government. His fruits and vegetables were judged to be outstanding in appearance, flavor, and nutritional value. The news headline read as follows:

Vocabulary Skills

Write the words from the story that have these meanings.

1. a shortage; being without

_____
   Par. 1

2. always; again and again

_____
   Par. 2

3. a sudden feeling of fear or uneasiness

_____
   Par. 3

Choose the word that correctly completes each sentence and write it in the blank.

4. Frederick wanted to _____ the sound of his own footsteps. (hear, here)

5. Frederick didn't _____ just where to find dirt, but he kept looking. (know, no)

6. He heard the jingling of a few _____ in his pocket. (cents, sense)

7. To stand on the ground in _____ feet was Frederick's dream. (bare, bear)

Use the underlined words in each sentence to form a compound word.

8. The light from the sun is called

_____.

9. The roof at the top of a building is the _____.

Reading Skills

1. Where does this story take place?

_____

2. What is Frederick's dream?

_____

_____

3. What is Frederick's secret?

_____

_____

Study Skills

Number each list of words below in alphabetical order.

1. _____ stale
   _____ buildings
   _____ still
   _____ breathe

2. _____ dirt
   _____ garden
   _____ mix
   _____ ground

3. _____ patch
   _____ surface
   _____ courage
   _____ streets

4. _____ thump
   _____ soft
   _____ stomping
   _____ standing

Buildings: From Tall to Taller

Read to find out about tall buildings.

1   Looking up at them might make you dizzy. Looking down from the top of them might make you dizzy, too. Tall buildings are a wonder, whether looking up or down.

Two Ways to Get Tall

2   Today's skyscrapers trace their roots all the way back to the 1880s. During that decade, two things happened. First, a man named William Jenney had the idea of using a steel frame to hold up the walls and floors of a building. Then, he added just a thin "skin" for the outer walls—instead of heavy stone or brick—to enclose the building. Jenney's design made it possible to make larger, taller buildings.

3   The second thing that happened was that elevator design improved. This, too, made it possible to make buildings taller.

How Tall Is Tall?

4   Back in 1883, Jenney's first tall building was 10 stories high. Imagine what he would think of today's skyscrapers, topping out at 110 stories.

5   Tall buildings are measured from the sidewalk level at the front entrance. At the top, spires are measured, but antennae and flag poles do not count. In 2004, a new building took first place on the list. Taipei 101, at 1,670 feet tall, beats the previous first-place winner by 187 feet.

Vocabulary Skills

Match each word in the first list with its antonym, or opposite, in the second list. Write the letter in the blank.

1. _____ short   a. thick

2. _____ thin   b. tall

3. _____ heavy   c. front

4. _____ back   d. light

For each word below, draw a line to divide the word into syllables.

5. e a g e r

6. h e a v y

7. s e c o n d

8. d e s i g n

9. l e v e l

Reading Skills

1. The author's purpose was probably to

   _____ entertain.

   _____ give information.

   _____ persuade.

2. Improvements in elevator design made it possible to build taller buildings because _____

   _____

   _____.

Study Skills

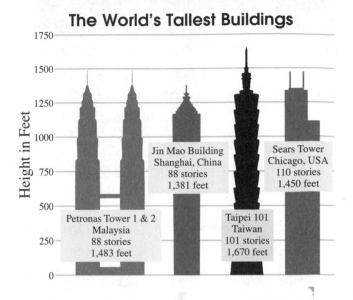

The World's Tallest Buildings

Height in Feet

1750
1500
1250
1000
750
500
250
0

Petronas Tower 1 & 2
Malaysia
88 stories
1,483 feet

Jin Mao Building
Shanghai, China
88 stories
1,381 feet

Taipei 101
Taiwan
101 stories
1,670 feet

Sears Tower
Chicago, USA
110 stories
1,450 feet

1. In general, what does the graph show?

   _____

   _____

2. Find one fact that appears in both the text and on the graph.

   _____

   _____

3. Name one fact that you found on the graph but that is not found in the text.

   _____

   _____

Magic With Flowers

What are Josh and Gary trying to do?

1   "*Ala-ka-ZAM!*" said Gary, trying to make his voice sound big. He waved his arms in and out in what he hoped was a fancy pattern, then tapped the box sitting on the table with a magic wand. He held his breath. The box jiggled a little. Then, the table jiggled a little.

2   "*Ahhhhh!*" The exclamation erupted from under the table.

3   "What's the matter?" called Gary. "Did it work?"

4   Gary's friend Josh came out from under the table. His hair was wet. His shirt was wet. He was holding a vase of fake flowers. "Well, it worked if you don't count spilling water all over," Josh grumbled. The boys had put water in the vase because they thought it would make it all seem more real.

5   "Maybe we should use real flowers," suggested Gary.

6   "They'd just wilt," Josh shook his head.

7   Gary shrugged. "Yeah, I guess so. Aside from spilling, how did it go under there?"

8   Josh told what had happened. When Gary tapped the box, Josh was supposed to open the secret door on the bottom of the box and pull the vase of flowers down, then close up the box again. But the bottom had gotten stuck and the vase had tipped. The boys sat down to rethink their plan.

9   The boys had thought the old broken table was almost too good to be true. Its worn-out wicker top had a hole that was just the right size for covering with the box as well as making stuff disappear by pulling it downward.

10   "This whole magic thing just isn't as easy as I thought it would be," noted Gary.

11   "Yeah, I know," Josh agreed. "How do you suppose the real magicians did it? They made stuff disappear all the time."

12   An idea popped into Gary's head and his face brightened. "Maybe it is the fake flowers. The real ones used real stuff, like rabbits. We need a rabbit. Go get Wiggles!"

Vocabulary Skills

Write the words from the story that have these meanings.

1. not plain

_____
Par. 1

2. flowing from a container

_____
Par. 4

3. droop

_____
Par. 6

4. jammed; caught in a position

_____
Par. 8

Form the plural of each word below by adding **s** or **es**. Write the word on the line.

5. arm _____

6. table _____

7. branch _____

8. vase _____

9. box _____

10. flower _____

The prefix **re-** means "again." So, *redo* means "do again." Use the words below to complete each sentence. Write the words in the blanks.

reappear	reinvent	rethink

11. The boys wished they could _____ what the great magicians had done.

12. "If we do make something go away, I wonder how we make it _____," wondered Gary.

13. When their trick didn't work, the boys sat down to _____ the plan.

Reading Skills

1. This story is mostly about

_____ two boys trying to do a magic trick.

_____ a boy teaching another boy a magic trick.

_____ how to do a magic trick.

2. Josh got wet because _____

_____.

3. Why was Josh under the table?

_____

_____

4. What do you think will happen next?

_____

_____

_____

Magic With Wiggles

Read to see whether Josh and Gary's new trick works.

1   *Well, okay*, thought Josh. Every magician they had ever read about had used rabbits. Josh couldn't believe they hadn't thought of Wiggles earlier. He had a good feeling about this.

2   Gary put a lettuce leaf in the box, then Josh put Wiggles in the box and closed one of the top flaps. Josh got into position under the table so he could pull Wiggles through the hole in the bottom of the box and make him disappear.

3   Gary cleared his throat and raised his arms slowly. *"Ala-ka-...."*

4   "Hey, wait," called Josh from underneath the table. He crawled part way out. "Maybe we should try a new word. A rabbit-y word."

5   "A rabbit-y word?" Gary looked doubtful. "Like what?"

6   "Well, I don't know." Josh thought for a moment. "How about *rabbit-o-zam*?

7   *"Rabbit-o-ZAM!"* Gary tried it out. Both boys shook their heads.

8   Josh tried again. *"Shish-rabbit-ka-zam!"* Nope.

9   *"Abra-ca-DAB-rabbit!"* tried Gary.

10   *"Abra-ca-DAB-rabbit?"* Josh was laughing so hard he could barely get the word out.

11   After a good laughing spell, the boys got back down to business. They agreed to go back to good old *abracadabra*.

12   Josh took his position, and Gary did his part, complete with arms, cape waving, and stick tapping. The box jiggled a tiny bit. The table jiggled.

13   *"Ahhhhh!"* The cry from under the table was truly alarming

14   "Now what's wrong?" cried Gary.

15   *"It worked!"* screamed Josh, scrambling out from under the table. *"It worked! Wiggles is gone!"*

16   "It worked?" cried Gary, and he dived under the table in disbelief. When he came out, the boys did a little dance, then they bowed to the imaginary crowd, quite certain that they heard wild clapping.

17   Wiggles had, indeed, disappeared.

Vocabulary Skills

Write the words from the story that have these meanings.

1. at a time before

   _____
   Par. 1

2. moved on hands and knees

   _____
   Par. 4

3. shared the same view

   _____
   Par. 11

A **contraction** is one word that stands for two words. Write a contraction for each pair of words below.

4. could not _____

5. she will _____

6. what is _____

7. he would _____

8. Now write a sentence using the contraction you wrote for question 4, above.

   _____

   _____

   _____

In each row below, circle the three words that belong together.

9. snake   rabbit   hamster   mouse

10. cape   hat   wand   briefcase

11. garden   tree   table   grass

Reading Skills

1. How was the magic trick supposed to work?

   _____

   _____

2. What actually happened?

   _____

   _____

Write the best word to complete each sentence below.

3. They should have thought of Wiggles _____. (brighter, sooner, calmer)

4. The magic words made the boys _____ so hard. (laugh, lame, learn)

5. It made Gary feel like a real magician when he _____ his cape. (waved, cried, tapped)

6. The boys couldn't _____ Wiggles was gone. (agree, scramble, believe)

7. Write **R** next to the sentences that tell about something real. Write **M** next to the sentences that are about made-up things.

   _____ Rabbits eat lettuce.

   _____ Rabbits disappear and reappear.

   _____ Magicians say magic words.

Houdini

What made Harry Houdini so great?

1   Do you believe in magic? The greatest magician of all time didn't. Harry Houdini was known as "The King of Cards" and "The Great Escape Artist." But he was the first to say that his magic tricks were tricks, not magic.

2   Houdini's early interest in magic tricks led him to read about famous magicians. He studied, then practiced and practiced. His first magic shows, begun when he was 17, included mostly card tricks. He added new tricks, such as escaping from an ordinary box, once he had perfected them.

3   From those simple beginnings, Houdini's magic tricks became more showy and more daring. He escaped from handcuffs. Then, he allowed audience members to bring their own handcuffs to prove he could escape from *any* pair of handcuffs. Then, he escaped from a straightjacket, hanging upside down by his ankles.

4   How can a performer top his own top performance? Think of a trick that seems truly impossible. He had himself locked into a crate and thrown into a river. He also had himself sealed into a lead coffin, which was placed into a hotel swimming pool. An hour later, Houdini waved to the waiting fans and newspaper reporters.

5   Houdini strongly supported the work of magicians but just as strongly spoke against "fake" magicians who claimed that they had special powers or communicated with "spirits." Houdini would expose these false magicians by visiting their shows, then writing magazine or newspaper articles to reveal how they fooled their audiences.

6   To set himself apart from the "spiritual" magicians, Houdini practiced his tricks, perfected them, then practiced again. Though Harry Houdini died more than 75 years ago, the man and his tricks have never been matched.

Vocabulary Skills

Write the words from the article that have these meanings.

1. well known

   _____
   Par. 2

2. getting away, breaking out

   _____
   Par. 2

3. making or having a big display

   _____
   Par. 3

4. not true

   _____
   Par. 5

Circle the word that correctly completes each sentence. Write the word in the blank.

5. Most people would _____ Houdini was the greatest.

   train   say   play

6. What do you _____ about in your spare time?

   read   clean   sweep

7. It must be hard to think up your _____ tricks.

   crown   own   round

8. They _____ for Houdini to come out of the coffin.

   shaped   paid   waited

Reading Skills

1. The author wrote this article to

   _____ persuade.

   _____ make you laugh.

   _____ give you information.

Write **F** next to each sentence that is a fact. Write **O** next to each sentence that is an opinion.

2. _____ Harry Houdini died more than 75 years ago.

3. _____ Houdini could escape from handcuffs.

4. _____ Harry Houdini was the only "real" magician.

5. _____ Houdini's magic tricks were wonderful.

Study Skills

You could learn about Harry Houdini by looking under "H" for Houdini or "M" for magic.

Look at these topics. Write where you could learn more in an encyclopedia. The first one is done for you.

robins __R (robin)__   __B (bird)__

1. light bulbs _____ _____

2. corn _____ _____

David Copperfield

What kind of a magician is David Copperfield?

1   An illusion is something that fools the senses or the mind. An illusion may make you think something exists when it really does not. It may be something that appears to be one thing, but is really something else. David Copperfield calls himself an *illusionist.* He is someone who makes or creates illusions.

2   Many people are interested in magic, but most of them are not performing and getting paid for it by age 12. Nor are they teaching college-level classes in magic at age 16. Copperfield was the youngest person ever to be allowed to join the Society of American Magicians. When he got to college himself, Copperfield got the leading part in a play called *The Magic Man.* In addition to acting and singing, he created all the magic in the show.

The show ran for longer than any other musical in Chicago's history.

3   Copperfield is a huge success as a showy illusionist, but he has other projects as well. He says that his best work is Project Magic. Copperfield developed a number of tricks done with the hands. These tricks help hospital patients who need to improve their hand strength or coordination, the ability to move and control their fingers. Learning to do the tricks also builds confidence. Patients in the program can boast that they can do tricks that able-bodied people can't do.

4   Like many magicians, Copperfield has an interest in the history of magic. He has created a museum and library in which books, articles, and old magic props, or equipment, are stored and displayed. By keeping track of history, Copperfield hopes to save magic for future generations.

Vocabulary Skills

Write the words from the article that have these meanings.

1. putting on an act

   _____
   Par. 2

2. to become a member of

   _____
   Par. 2

3. invented; created

   _____
   Par. 3

4. belief in oneself

   _____
   Par. 3

The ending **-ist** means "one who does" or "one who practices." An *illusionist* is "one who practices, or makes, illusions." Add **ist** to the following words. Use the new words to complete the sentences.

arbor	special

5. After much study, he became a(n) _____ in his field.

6. The Latin word for "tree" is *arbor*, so a(n) _____ is someone who cares for trees.

Reading Skills

1. David Copperfield is an

   _____.

2. What did he start doing at age 12?

   _____

3. What was he doing by age 16?

   _____

Check all answers that are correct.

4. Which of these words do you think best describe Copperfield?

   _____ thoughtless

   _____ lazy

   _____ hard-working

   _____ talented

5. What do you think a magician could learn from Copperfield's collection of old magic books and equipment?

   _____

   _____

   _____

6. If you were a magician or an illusionist, what kinds of tricks would you like to do?

   _____

   _____

Study Skills

1. The headings below belong in this article. To which paragraph does each heading belong?

   Copperfield's Beginnings _____

   What Is an Illusion? _____

   Saving Magic for the Future _____

   Project Magic _____

Wiggles Reappears

How do the boys get Wiggles back?

1 "Which word do you think did it?" asked Josh.

2 "What do you mean?" said Gary, still feeling great because their magic trick had worked. They had finally gotten something to disappear.

3 "Was it *shish-rabbit-ka-zam* or *abra-ca-dab-rabbit*?" Josh asked, working hard to repeat the magic words they had thought up.

4 Gary laughed again, remembering the words. "Oh, I think it was definitely *abra-ca-dab-rabbit*, don't you?"

5 "I don't know," shrugged Josh. "I guess we'll have to try each of them backwards to get him back."

6 All of a sudden it was very quiet. Gary looked at Josh. How in the world were they going to get Wiggles back?

7 "I think I remember all the words," Gary said, trying to encourage Josh. Wiggles was Josh's pet, after all.

8 The boys sat down on the back steps of Josh's house to figure out how to say the words backwards so the magic would work the other way.

9 "Okay," said Gary, thinking hard. "We have *zam-ka-rabbit-shish* and *rabbit-dab-ca-abra*."

10 Josh continued, "And *zam-o-rabbit* and just plain old *dabra-ca-abra*."

11 Gary nodded, "I think that's it."

12 "*Ahhhhh!*" The cry came from around the corner of the house. It was Josh's mom.

13 "Mom? What's the matter?" called Josh as both boys went running.

14 "Now how many times have I told you not to chew on my..." Josh heard his mom's voice. Just around the corner, both boys stopped short.

15 "Wiggles! He reappeared!" Josh cried.

16 Mom looked at the boys. "Wiggles? Reappeared? Who's going to make my flowers reappear?"

17 The boys looked at each other, smiled, and nodded. They waved their arms and said, in their best magician voices, "*Zam-ka-flowers-SHISH!*"

Vocabulary Skills

Add an **'s** at the end of a word to show that something belongs to someone. Add **'s** to each name. Then, write the name in the correct blank.

Josh	Gary	Mom

1. _____ flowers

2. _____ pet rabbit

3. _____ cape

Reading Skills

1. Number the sentences to show the order in which events happened in the story.

   _____ Gary laughed about their magic words.

   _____ The boys heard Josh's mom.

   _____ The boys discovered Mom and Wiggles.

   _____ The boys figured out how to say the words backwards.

   _____ Gary felt great because their trick worked.

   _____ The boys tried to make Mom's flowers reappear.

Circle the name or names that each underlined word, or **pronoun**, stands for.

2. "I think I remember all the words," Gary said.

   Josh   Gary   Wiggles

3. "Wiggles! He reappeared!" Josh cried.

   Josh   Gary   Wiggles

Study Skills

Number each list of words below in alphabetical order.

1. _____ trick

   _____ magic

   _____ disappear

   _____ word

2. _____ backwards

   _____ guess

   _____ going

   _____ pet

3. _____ how

   _____ house

   _____ way

   _____ other

4. _____ steps

   _____ voice

   _____ rabbit

   _____ reappear

Field Trip

What do the children see during their bus ride?

1 The crisp wind tore at the children. They held their jackets out, letting them puff up with air. The October wind only added to the excitement. Today was a field trip day. The children were in line, being counted before they got onto the rumbling yellow bus. Counting was taking a long time because of the movement of the wind and the children.

2 At last they were on the bus, two to a seat, sometimes three. A few parents spread themselves out and settled in for the noisy, bumpy ride.

3 As the trip began, Mrs. Mason and Steven were playing riddley-riddley-ree in the front seat when Jason tapped their shoulders and pointed. "Oh, look at that cute building," he cried.

4 Mrs. Mason turned her attention out the window. "This is a little town called Rockville," she said. "It's been here for more than 150 years. Some of those cute buildings are that old."

5 "Wow!" said Steven. "What's in them?"

6 "Well, I see a hardware store, a grocery store, a card shop, a diner..."

7 "And there's a candle shop and a shoe store," added Jason. He, Jesse, and Steven named all the stores they saw. It was easy because there weren't really very many. All of a sudden, the bus was rolling along between tall, dry cornfields waiting to be harvested.

8 "Well," said Jason, "that really was a little town."

9 Riddley-riddley-ree continued and it was a while before anyone really looked out the window. Riddley-riddley-ree wasn't fair, after all, unless you named something that was inside the bus that everyone could see.

10 When he did look out the window again, Steven saw a long gray wall. It went on and on beside the bus on both sides of the highway. It was so tall that he couldn't see over it. *What could be behind that wall?* Steven wondered.

Vocabulary Skills

Write the words from the story that have these meanings.

1. rough, bouncy

   _____
   Par. 2

2. store that sells food

   _____
   Par. 6

3. gathered a crop

   _____
   Par. 7

4. according to the rules

   _____
   Par. 9

Make a check next to the meaning that fits the underlined word in each sentence.

5. Be careful not to <u>trip</u> on the rock.

   _____ to stumble

   _____ a journey

6. One building was a <u>store</u>.

   _____ to collect and save items

   _____ a place to buy things

7. Each house had its own <u>well</u>.

   _____ a hole dug for water

   _____ an exclamation

8. The children did not have a <u>fair</u> day for their field trip.

   _____ light-colored, as hair or skin

   _____ sunny and clear, without wind

Reading Skills

1. The children notice that the town of Rockville is _____.

2. What three sights do the children see out the bus window? Write the parts of the sentences from the story that tell you.

   _____

   _____

   _____

The place where a story happens is the **setting**. An author might describe how a place looks, how it feels, or how it smells. The author of this story described the setting of this story in the first paragraph. Answer these questions.

3. During what time of year does this story take place?

   _____

4. What kind of day is it?

   _____

5. What detail tells you that it might be a little chilly?

   _____

Spectrum Reading Grade 3

89

Riddles Along the Way

What ideas do the children have about the wall?

1 "What do you think it's for?" Steven asked Jason and Jesse in the seat behind him. They looked out the bus window where Steven was pointing. They saw the long gray wall that went on like a snake beside them.

2 Jesse had an idea. "Maybe there's a lake on the other side of it," she guessed.

3 "But it's been going on for ages," said Steven. "I didn't think there were any lakes that big around here. Besides, it's on both sides of the road." Jason and Jesse whirled around to the windows on the far side of the bus.

4 "Oh, I guess you're right," Jesse shrugged. "There wouldn't be lakes on both sides of the road, would there?"

5 "Maybe there are castles on both sides of the road," suggested Jason. "And maybe the people who live in the castles built the walls because they don't get along with each other."

6 Steven and Jesse looked at Jason in shock. Then, Jason smiled and held up a book he'd been reading. Its title was *The Truth about Castles, Knights, and Moats*. Steven and Jesse laughed along with Jason.

7 When he could talk again, Steven said, "For a minute there, I thought you had gone completely nuts."

8 Jason grinned. "Yeah, I could tell." Then, he looked out the window again. "So what do you think it's for?" Mrs. Mason, who had been talking to someone across the aisle, heard the question.

9 "You're wondering about the wall?" she asked. "There are houses on the other side. The wall blocks the highway noise so the people who live there can have a quiet neighborhood."

10 "So my idea was half right," pointed out Jason matter-of-factly. "The people built the walls because they didn't get along with the highway."

Vocabulary Skills

Match each word in the first list with its antonym in the second list. Write the letter in the blank.

1. _____ behind   **a.** ahead

2. _____ noise   **b.** loud

3. _____ long   **c.** silence

4. _____ quiet   **d.** short

Form a contraction from each pair of words below. Write the contraction.

5. it is _____

6. there is _____

7. did not _____

8. would not _____

9. you are _____

10. do not _____

Reading Skills

Write **T** if the sentence is true. Write **F** if the sentence is false.

1. _____ The children saw a castle.

2. _____ The wall was on only one side of the bus.

3. _____ Jason had a book on the bus.

4. _____ The walls surrounded a lake.

5. What does this story tell you about Jason? You may check more than one.

_____ He likes to joke around.

_____ He is interested in history.

_____ He doesn't get along with Steven.

_____ He has never been on a field trip before.

Study Skills

In a dictionary, you will find two words at the top of each page. These are **guide words**. The first guide word shows what the first entry on the page is. The last guide word is the last entry word on the page. All the other words on the page fall in alphabetical order between the two guide words.

Look at the guide words below. Then, check the words that would fall on that dictionary page.

wall / whisper

1. _____ wet

2. _____ wax

3. _____ wick

4. _____ west

5. _____ worth

6. _____ wrist

7. _____ waffle

8. _____ wilt

One Great Wall

Where is the Great Wall of China and why was it built?

1   A wall has many uses. It may hold things in. It may keep things out. It may hold things up. In the case of China's Great Wall, the purpose was to keep things out. Tribes of people wanted to move across China's northern mountains and down into China. China's emperors preferred to keep those people out of China. So, four different walls started going up as early as 700 B.C.

2   About 500 years later, the emperor got tired of fighting off the northern tribes. He wanted to connect the four main sections of the wall that had already been built. He sent thousands of peasants, poor people who did not have farms, to work on the wall. Soldiers were there to make sure the peasants stayed and worked. They did work hard, and many of them died.

3   Then, 1,500 years after that, another emperor wanted to make the wall even stronger. He started a program that lasted more than 200 years! The wall got longer, and watch-towers and cannons were added at points all along the length of the wall.

4   In spite of the wall, China did suffer a number of invasions over the years. Still, the wall's size and the human effort that went into it earn it a place on the list of greatest human feats.

The Facts on the Great Wall

Length	1,500 mi.
Width	15–30 ft. at base; 12 ft. at top
Height	25 ft. (average)
Materials	bricks, rocks, packed earth

Vocabulary Skills

Circle the word that is a synonym of the underlined word in each sentence.

1. It was a huge job to <u>connect</u> the old parts of the wall.

   join   build   move

2. Building the wall must have been hard <u>work</u>.

   faith   strength   labor

3. Even with the wall, China was <u>invaded</u> a number of times.

   improved   built   attacked

4. What else can you think of that is a great human <u>feat</u>?

   building   accomplishment   wall

Write the correct abbreviation in each blank.

mi.   ft.

5. If you are standing on the Great Wall, you could be about 25 _____ above the ground.

6. The top of the wall was made 12 _____ wide so soldiers and carts could travel along the wall.

7. If every curve of the wall is measured, it is 1,500 _____ long.

8. If a straight line were drawn from one end of the wall to the other, the line would be 1,200 _____ long.

Reading Skills

1. The Great Wall of China was built

   _____ as a place for soldiers to live.

   _____ to protect China.

   _____ to honor the emperors.

Write the best word to complete each sentence below.

2. It took hundreds of years to _____ the Great Wall of China. (move, build, climb)

3. Peasants were poor _____ who did not have farms. (people, emperors, walls)

4. Today, people may _____ the Great Wall and walk along it. (twist, visit, hear)

Study Skills

1. What does the map show?

   _____

   _____

2. Based on the map, describe how the Great Wall might look from high above earth.

   _____

   _____

A Wall of Names

Why was this wall built?

1   Most walls draw lines between people or things. One wall in Washington, D.C., is meant to invite people to come close. Rather than separate people, it is supposed to draw people together.

2   The low black stone wall that makes up the Vietnam Veterans Memorial stretches along a green grassy slope. The 58,245 names carved into the wall are the names of men and women who died or went missing while serving in the U.S. Armed Forces during the Vietnam War.

3   The committee that was raising money and organizing the memorial held a contest to find a design. They had four requirements. The design for the memorial had to

    1. be thoughtful.

    2. fit in with its surroundings.

    3. contain the names of all those who died during the Vietnam conflict or were still missing.

    4. make no political statement about the war.

More than 1,400 design ideas were sent to the committee. From all those ideas, the design of a college student, Maya Ying Lin, was chosen. Construction was completed in 1982.

4   Tens of thousands of people visit the wall each year. Some of them knew people whose names are on the wall. Others visit just to see, and perhaps to remember the 1960s, when Americans hotly disagreed about the war. The wall, though, is not a war memorial, but a memorial to those who served in the war, both living and dead. No matter what one thinks of the Vietnam War, 2.7 million American military people worked hard in difficult conditions, and thousands of them lost their lives. That deserves to be remembered.

Vocabulary Skills

Write the words from the article that have these meanings.

1. divide, keep apart

   _____
   Par. 1

2. small or gentle hill

   _____
   Par. 2

3. had different opinions

   _____
   Par. 4

Circle the correct letters to complete each word. Write the letters in the blank.

4. The people whose names are on the wall all s_____ved during the Vietnam War.

         ir   er   ur

5. The names are c_____ved into the black stone.

         or   ar   er

Reading Skills

1. This article is mostly about

   _____ Maya Ying Lin.

   _____ the Vietnam War.

   _____ the Vietnam Veterans Memorial.

2. The Wall was completed in

   _____.

3. How many names are on the wall?

   _____

4. Why was the Vietnam Veterans Memorial built?

   _____

   _____

5. Look at the picture of the wall. Then, look back at the design requirements. Write how you think the Wall meets one of those requirements.

   _____

   _____

   _____

Study Skills

In what volume of the encyclopedia would you look to find these topics? Write the volume number.

1. China _____

2. Washington, D.C. _____

3. castles _____

4. dams _____

5. moats _____

6. invasions _____

A Farm from Long Ago

What will the students learn about at the farm?

1   When the bus stopped, everyone filed out and waited under some large shade trees. Jesse and Steven practiced making wings out of their jackets.

2   "Wow!" said Steven over the wind. "It's even more windy here than it was at school!"

3   Just then, Jesse noticed a woman coming from the big white house. She wore a dress that dragged on the grass. On her head was a small white cap, tied under her chin. Jesse was amazed at how different her own shirt, jeans and sneakers were from the woman's.

4   Mrs. Mason spoke to the woman for a minute, then motioned for the students to gather around and listen.

5   "Welcome to Fairfield Farm, children," began the smiling woman. "My name is Mrs. Hoff, and my job is to help you learn about what life was like many years ago."

6   "Hello, Mrs. Hoff," the students echoed.

7   "First, let me tell you a little bit about Fairfield Farm. The Owen family started this farm about 140 years ago. Most of the tools and machines that you will see on the farm today are from the 1860s." Just then, a gust of wind caught at Mrs. Hoff's full skirt and nearly pushed her backward. The students giggled.

8   "You will notice," Mrs. Hoff continued, "that life in the 1860s was a little different than it is now. I notice that every time I put this dress on and come to work." Mrs. Hoff grinned, and the students giggled again. "But there are many wonderful things to learn from how farmers and their families lived and worked all those years ago.

9   "Now, I'd like half of you to come with me to the barn first. The rest of you will go with Mrs. Mason to see what's happening in the farm kitchen. Okay?" With a swing of her skirt, Mrs. Hoff set off toward the barn. Jesse and Jason waved to Steven as their groups separated. Jesse crossed her fingers and hoped for lots of animals in the barn.

Vocabulary Skills

Use the words below to complete the sentences. Use each word twice.

wind	spoke

1. Don't forget to _____ the clock.

2. When Mrs. Hoff _____, everyone listened.

3. My bicycle wheel has a broken _____.

4. I like to hear the _____ in the trees.

To show that something happened in the past, most words add **ed** to the end. Some words, however, don't follow that pattern. For example, the past form of *sing* is *sang*. Use the words below to complete the sentences.

catch—caught
teach—taught
freeze—froze

5. Mrs. Hoff will _____ us about the farm, just as she was _____ to do.

6. Did it _____ last night? I nearly _____ while I waited for the bus this morning.

7. I would like to _____ the wind, but I think it _____ me first.

Reading Skills

1. What kind of day is it?

_____

2. What are the children going to learn about?

_____

_____

3. How is Jesse's clothing different from Mrs. Hoff's?

_____

_____

_____

4. Have you ever been on a field trip? What kinds of things did you do?

_____

_____

_____

_____

5. What do you think will happen next?

_____

_____

_____

_____

In the Barn

What do the students learn about in the barn?

1   Jesse could hear the noises even before they got to the barn. There were definitely animals in there.

2   "Jason, do you think we'll see cows, horses, or what?" she asked excitedly.

3   "I'm hoping for geese, myself," answered Jason. He flapped his arms and made a honking sound.

4   When they stepped into the barn, Jesse saw a man standing by a fence talking to some animals. *Excellent!* thought Jesse, *I forgot about sheep!* The man had on an old brown hat, a light brown shirt, brown pants, and heavy brown boots.

5   "Hello, Mr. Brown. How are you today?" Mrs. Hoff sang out.

6   Jesse giggled. *Well, what else could his name be?* she thought to herself.

7   The man touched his hat in an old-fashioned way to greet Mrs. Hoff.

8   "I was just checking to see how the wool was growing," said Mr. Brown.

9   "Does wool really grow?" asked one of the students.

10   "Why, sure it does," Mr. Brown replied. "I clipped these sheep just about down to the skin in spring. Now just look how wooly they are. By next spring, they'll have a nice crop of wool for me to clip off again."

11   Jason had a question. "What happens to it then?"

12   Mr. Brown marked off the steps on his fingers. "First, the wool gets washed. Then, it gets cleaned and fluffed, or carded, then dyed. Next, the wool gets spun into yarn. Then, someone weaves it into cloth. In fact, these clothes I'm wearing are made of wool from these very sheep."

13   Jesse couldn't wait any more. "Do the sheep have names?"

14   "Oh, yes," said Mr. Brown, turning toward the sheep. "This is Socks. This is Pants. There's Shirt. Over here is Yarn, and this one is Coat."

15   Jesse caught the twinkle in Mr. Brown's eyes and smiled at him. *Well, what else could their names be?*

Vocabulary Skills

When a short word has an **ing** ending, the syllable break comes between the word and its ending. If the final consonant is doubled, as in *stepping*, the syllables break between the double consonant: *step/ping*. For each word below, draw a line to divide the word into syllables.

1. f l a p p i n g
2. h o n k i n g
3. s t a n d i n g
4. t i p p i n g
5. g r o w i n g

Reading Skills

1. In the barn, the students saw _____.

In this story, the author uses **dialogue** to move the story along. For each piece of dialogue below, fill in the name of the character who said it. Then, write what the dialogue tells you about the character or the story.

2. "I was just checking to see how the wool was growing."

_____

_____

3. "Does wool really grow?"

_____

_____

_____

4. "I clipped these sheep just about down to the skin in spring."

_____

_____

_____

5. Write **R** next to the sentences that tell about something real. Write **M** next to the sentences that are about made-up things.

_____ Farmers raise sheep.

_____ A sheep's coat is wool.

_____ Sheep come in many bright colors, just like yarn.

6. Number the sentences to show the order in which wool is processed.

_____ Card the wool.

_____ Weave the wool.

_____ Clip the wool.

_____ Spin the wool.

_____ Wash the wool.

_____ Dye the wool.

Spectrum Reading Grade 3

99

In the Kitchen

What does Steven learn in the kitchen?

1   Steven couldn't believe the smell coming from the kitchen as he walked across the back porch. It was great.

2   Mrs. Mason held the squeaky screen door open. Steven and the rest of the group went through it. *Ahhh,* thought Steven, *fresh bread!*

3   Inside the big square kitchen was a big wooden table. On the far side was a huge stove. Above it was a round pipe going up, then out through the wall. A woman dressed almost like Mrs. Hoff was standing behind the table. There was one difference though. This woman had her sleeves rolled up. It was hot in this kitchen. The woman began talking just as if they had been there all along.

4   "When the Owens ran this farm in the 1860s, Saturday would have been bread-baking day. A farm wife baked a week's worth of bread for her family and any hired hands that lived at the farm." While she talked, she kept right on pulling and pushing a huge mound of bread dough on the table.

5   "Did anyone notice that it's rather warm in here?" the woman asked.

6   "I sure did!" answered Steven right away. His classmates nodded their heads.

7   "That's one of the reasons a farm wife baked bread only once a week. It's quite a process, and it means that the kitchen is really going to heat up," explained the woman. She brushed some hair back with her arm.

8   "Speaking of heat, the stove is hungry again." She looked up at the students. "Would each of you go and get a piece of wood from the porch to fill my wood box? Then, we'll slice one of these loaves and see how the bread turned out. Okay?"

9   *With pleasure,* thought Steven, and he led the way out to the woodpile on the porch.

Vocabulary Skills

In each row below, circle the three words that belong together.

1. stove   sink   oven   bed

2. cow   house   barn   shed

3. bread   apple   roll   muffin

Write the words from the story that have these meanings.

4. making a short, high-pitched sound

   _____
   Par. 2

5. the part of clothing that covers the arms

   _____
   Par. 3

6. cooked in an oven

   _____
   Par. 4

7. to cut something into thin pieces

   _____
   Par. 8

Use the underlined words in each sentence to form a compound word. Write the word on the line.

8. The <u>pile</u> of <u>wood</u> is on the porch.

   _____

9. The <u>house</u> is at the center of the <u>farm</u>.

   _____

10. After plowing all day, the farmer had an <u>ache</u> in his <u>back</u>.

   _____

Reading Skills

1. It's hot in the kitchen because

   _____.

2. What does the woman mean when she says, "the stove is hungry"?

   _____

   _____

3. Is Steven eager to taste the bread? How can you tell?

   _____

   _____

Write **F** next to each sentence that is a fact. Write **O** next to each sentence that is an opinion.

4. _____ Some people still bake their own bread.

5. _____ Bread is best when baked in a wood stove.

6. _____ All bread smells good when it's baking.

Circle the name or names that each underlined word, or **pronoun**, stands for.

7. Steven couldn't believe the smell coming from the kitchen as <u>he</u> walked across the back porch.

   Steven   smell   kitchen

8. Mrs. Mason held the squeaky screen door open. Steven and the rest of the group went through <u>it</u>.

   Mrs. Mason   door   group

Baking Bread

Read to see what this newspaper article has to say about baking bread.

Baking Today

1 You may think that baking bread is a lost art. For one local woman, though, it is a daily event. Evelyn Seeley is the retired owner of A Loaf a Day bakery. Now that her grown children are running the bakery, Seeley has time to follow her own interests.

2 And what are her interests? Bread, of course! Almost every day, Seeley bakes a different kind of bread. She finds recipes among her many cookbooks, or she searches for them on her computer. "With the computer now, I don't think I'll ever run out of recipes," says Seeley. She doesn't think that she has repeated a recipe in her two years of retirement.

3 Seeley offers this recipe for our readers today. She says, "it's an oldie but a goody." Try it for yourself and see.

Sally Lunn Yeast Bread

1 pkg. dry yeast

$\frac{1}{4}$ c. warm water

6 T. butter

2 T. plus 1 tsp. sugar

2 eggs

$\frac{3}{4}$ c. milk

3 c. flour

$1\frac{1}{2}$ tsp. salt

4 Sprinkle yeast into the lukewarm water and set aside. In a bowl, cream butter and sugar. Beat in eggs. Blend in milk alternately with flour and salt. Beat after each addition. Then, add water and yeast. Beat until very smooth. Cover bowl and set in warm place. Let rise until double in bulk. Beat down with a wooden spoon and pour batter into a greased 9-in. tube pan. Let rise until just above edge of pan. Bake in preheated 350° F oven for 40–45 min.

Vocabulary Skills

Make a check next to the meaning that fits the underlined word in each sentence.

1. The recipe says to <u>cream</u> the butter and sugar.

_____ to beat or stir together

_____ thick, fatty part of milk

2. I hope I <u>bowl</u> well today.

_____ an open, usually round container

_____ a game played by rolling a ball down an alley

3. It is <u>kind</u> of Mrs. Seeley to share her bread.

_____ courteous or caring

_____ a group or type of something

4. Her quilt is filled with <u>down</u>.

_____ movement toward a lower level

_____ soft, fluffy feathers

Recipes often use short forms, or **abbreviations**, of words. Look at the common recipe words in the box. Write each word next to the correct item from the recipe.

cups	package
Fahrenheit	tablespoons
minutes	teaspoons

5. 40–45 min. _____

6. 6 T. butter _____

7. 350° F _____

8. 3 c. flour _____

9. I pkg. dry yeast _____

10. 1½ tsp. salt _____

Reading Skills

1. What did Evelyn Seeley do before she retired?

_____

_____

2. What does she do now that she's retired?

_____

_____

3. Number the sentences to show the order of the steps in the bread recipe.

_____ Add eggs.

_____ Let rise.

_____ Add milk, flour, and salt.

_____ Put yeast in water.

_____ Add yeast.

_____ Cream butter and sugar.

All About the Farm

What did the students like best about the farm?

1   "Jason! Did you see those geese?" Steven called to his friend as they got near the bus. The two boys had been in different groups during the class field trip. Now it was time to get on the bus and head back to school.

2   Jason waved to his friend. "I sure did. They were huge. One of them came right up to me, and he was as tall as my shoulder." Jason had really enjoyed the geese, and everyone around him could tell.

3   "I think they were my favorite, too," said Steven as he and Jason slid into a seat. In front of them, Jesse was telling Mrs. Mason about the sheep. "They were so fuzzy. Did you feel them?" Jesse wiggled her fingers in the air as if she were curling them into the sheep's wool.

4   Mrs. Mason laughed. "I know what you mean, Jesse. It made me want to curl up inside the pen with the sheep."

5   Steven nodded. "I think the sheep might have been my favorite, too, Jesse."

6   "What about you, Mrs. Mason?" asked Jesse. "What was your favorite part?"

7   "Oh, I loved all of it," she said, shaking her head. "If I had to pick just one thing, though, I would say…the bread…"

8   "Oh, the bread," broke in Jason as he hugged his stomach. "It was so warm."

9   "And sweet," added Jesse.

10   Everyone looked at Steven to get his reaction. He had a sort of dreamy smile on his face. "It was…perfect," was all he said.

Vocabulary Skills

Write the words from the story that have these meanings.

1. where the arms join the body

_____
Par. 2

2. moved across or sideways

_____
Par. 3

3. covered with a mass of hair or fur

_____
Par. 3

4. put one's arms around

_____
Par. 8

Match each word in the first list with its antonym in the second list. Write the letter in the blank.

5. _____ tall   **a.** sour

6. _____ huge   **b.** tiny

7. _____ different   **c.** same

8. _____ sweet   **d.** short

Write the past form of each action word below.

9. wave _____

10. laugh _____

11. love _____

12. enjoy _____

13. curl _____

Reading Skills

1. This story is mostly about

_____ what the students learned on their field trip.

_____ what the students liked best about the field trip.

_____ how much Jason liked the geese.

2. What is Jesse's favorite part about the farm?

_____

3. Which student seems unsure about his favorite part?

_____

4. How can you tell?

_____

_____

5. Would you say that Steven is hard to please or easy to please? Explain.

_____

_____

_____

6. Where are the characters when they have this conversation?

_____ in the barn

_____ in the kitchen

_____ on the bus

_____ outside

Caught in Traffic

What happens on the way back from the field trip?

1   Jason was winning. He and his friends had been trying to see who could list the most cool things that they had seen on the field trip. Jason had 27 so far. Steven was starting to catch up, though.

2   As Jesse thought up more ideas, she gazed out the bus window and realized that the bus wasn't moving. She saw long lines of cars beside them and stretching around a curve in front of them.

3   "Hey, I wonder what's happening," she said, pointing out the window. "Everyone is stopped."

4   The bus driver heard Jesse and nodded his head. "This often happens on the outer edges of the city, especially on Friday afternoons. Everyone has to be somewhere, and right now they're all right here," he said, turning to frown, but in a friendly way, at Jesse.

5   Jason was a little worried. "What if we don't get back to school on time?"

6   "Oh, we have plenty of time," Mrs. Mason quickly assured him. "And if it does get late, the bus driver can radio the school and let them know what's happening. It'll be all right."

7   "Just look at them all," said Jesse, still gazing out the window. "How many do you think there are?"

8   "Let's see!" suggested Steven. "One, two, three, four, five, six, seven, eight...."

9   "Okay, okay," cut in Jesse, waving a hand at Steven, "that's annoying." She grinned at Steven, and Steven grinned right back.

10   Jason had a different thought. "I wonder where they're all going and where they came from." The three friends all looked out the window at the cars disappearing into the distance. Each of them wondered about all the different kinds of people and all of their different reasons for being here right now, clogging up the highway.

Vocabulary Skills

These pairs of words sound the same, but have different meanings and spellings. Write the correct word from each pair to complete each sentence.

heard—herd	sea—see
know—no	sew—so

1. They could see _____ reason for the traffic jam.

2. Jason wondered why _____ many cars were here.

3. Jesse remembered the _____ of sheep at the farm.

4. She wished she could _____ them again.

The prefix **dis-** means "not." It causes a word to mean the opposite of its base word. For example, *disagree* means "not agree."

Add **dis** to the words below. Use the new words to complete the sentences.

appear	comfort	honest

5. To tell a lie is _____.

6. The bus driver wished the traffic would _____.

7. Sitting in traffic was annoying, but there was no real _____.

Sound out each syllable. Then, write the word and say it to yourself as you write.

8. dis/ap/pear/ing _____

9. an/noy/ing _____

10. af/ter/noon _____

Reading Skills

Write the best word to complete each sentence below.

1. Up ahead, the line of cars went around a _____. (curve, ledge, movement)

2. Jason was worried about the bus being _____. (hard, late, extra)

3. Steven wanted to _____ the cars. (spin, read, count)

4. Have you ever been stuck in traffic? Write about how it felt.

_____

_____

5. What might cause a traffic jam? List as many reasons as you can.

_____

_____

_____

_____

_____

_____

How Many Are There?

Read to see why we count things.

[1] Look in any newspaper and you are likely to see numbers. We like to know how many inches of rain we've had, or how many students are in our schools. We want to know how much the city government is spending, or how many people have voted. We like to see numbers.

[2] Fortunately, many people like to count or keep track of things. They count traffic accidents and help us decide where to put stop signs and traffic lights. They count people to help us decide when we need more houses or more schools. They count how many people catch the flu and tell us when to get shots.

[3] Some numbers help us see that we need to change something. Other numbers show us how things are changing. The numbers in the graph on this page show us how the population and the number of cars in the United States have changed. How has the growth in population affected or changed the United States? How has the increase in the number of cars affected the country? Think about how this growth has affected you and your community.

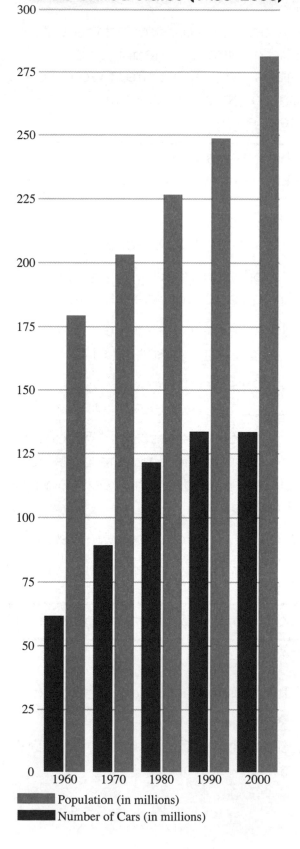

Population and Number of Cars in the United States (1960–2000)

Legend:
- Population (in millions)
- Number of Cars (in millions)

Vocabulary Skills

Write the words from the article that have these meanings.

1. paying out money

   _____
   Par. 1

2. unplanned events

   _____
   Par. 2

3. all of the people in an area

   _____
   Par. 3

Form the plural of each word.

4. number _____

5. inch _____

6. student _____

7. change _____

8. graph _____

Reading Skills

1. What kinds of things do we count? List two examples from the article.

   _____

   _____

2. What do we learn from counting things?

   _____

   _____

3. How do you think the information shown in this graph affects you and your community?

   _____

   _____

   _____

   _____

Study Skills

Use the bar graph to answer these questions.

1. For each year, which is greater, the population or the number of cars?

   _____

2. If you want population data for 1950, would this graph help you? How can you tell?

   _____

   _____

3. What was the population of the United States in 1970?

   _____

4. How many cars were there in 1990?

   _____

5. Which two bars on the graph are almost the same height?

   _____

   _____

Sidewalk Art

How do a sister and brother fill a long, hot afternoon?

1   I feel like a cactus. No, that's too dry. I feel like the glass greenhouse at the city park, all steamy and cloudy inside because the plants like it warm and moist. I feel like…

2   Oh, it's no use. I don't feel like anything. I'm just hot. It's hot outside. It's hot inside. There is nothing to do. I sit on the front steps of our building, trying to stay in a small triangle of shade. At the same time, I try to touch as little of the step as possible because everything feels hot and sticky, including my own skin.

3   I squint toward the sun to make bright, fuzzy patterns with my eyelashes. I watch a tree across the street. I can count on the fingers of one hand the number of leaves moving in the breeze. That's how weak the breeze is.

4   I try to think of something to do. I give myself a deadline. When the shade of my building gets to that crack in the sidewalk, I will do something. It happens slowly, just like everything else in the heat. When it gets close, I go down to the crack and watch. Yes, it's time. What should I do?

5   My brother Fujio's box of chalk is sitting forgotten at the bottom of the steps. I take out a piece of yellow chalk and make a blazing sun on the sidewalk. I surround it with white, then with every color in the chalk box.

6   Fujio appears at my side. "What's that, Tatsu?" he asks.

7   I don't say anything, but I write "Heat" at the bottom of my drawing. He just shrugs. Then, he gets the black chalk (his favorite color) and starts coloring. He fills a whole square of the sidewalk.

8   "What's that?" I ask.

9   "Shade," he says.

10   "Fujio, that's not…," I begin to say, but then I stop. It doesn't really matter. It's something to do, and that's a bonus on a hot day.

Vocabulary Skills

Circle the word that is a synonym of the underlined word in each sentence.

1. The plants like soil that is <u>moist</u>.

   shaken   dripping   damp

2. The breeze is so <u>weak</u> it doesn't do any good.

   faint   healthy   medium

3. The shade moved <u>close</u>.

   near   wide   quickly

Add **'s** at the end of a word to show that something belongs to someone. Add **'s** to each name. Then, write the name in the correct blank.

           Tatsu   Fujio

4. _____ chalk

5. _____ sun picture

Say *count*. Notice the sound that the letters **ou** make. Circle the word that has the same sound as **ou** in *count*.

6. show   cloudy   blow   close

7. drawing   should   outside   know

8. shower   could   flood   flow

9. crow   bloom   crown   would

Reading Skills

1. Tatsu is sitting in the shade on the front steps because _____

   _____.

2. Tatsu titles her drawing "Heat" because _____

   _____.

3. Write **R** next to the sentences that tell about something real. Write **M** next to the sentences that are about made-up things.

   _____ A person can make shade by drawing a picture of it.

   _____ A person can draw a picture of heat.

   _____ A person can draw a picture of the sun.

The **narrator** is the person who tells a story. Answer these questions.

4. Because the narrator is also a character, she uses the words *I* and *me* to tell her story. Find a place in the story where one of these words is used. Write the sentence here.

   _____

   _____

5. Where in the story do you discover what the narrator's name is?

   _____

   _____

Wishes on the Sidewalk

How do the children try to cool themselves off?

1   It's late afternoon now, and it's getting a little better. The heat, I mean. The shade came around to the front of the building, so at least the sidewalk doesn't burn you any more.

2   I tease Fujio about drawing a picture of shade. He's pretty cool about it. He just says, "It helped me think about not being hot."

3   I look at my own picture of the hot, hot sun. Maybe I should have tried it Fujio's way. Maybe my sun picture just makes it hotter here.

4   I see our neighbors Mario and Katie coming down the sidewalk. They stop and look at our pictures. Mario points at Fujio's black square and raises his eyebrows.

5   "Shade," sighs Fujio, as if he is tired of being an artist who is not understood. Mario wrinkles his brow for a moment, then bends down and picks up the blue chalk. He begins at a corner, just like Fujio did, and covers a square with blue.

6   It's too hot to talk, so we just wait. We figure he'll explain. When Mario is done, he stands up and gives a little bow. "Cool water," he says. Fujio and I smile. Then, Katie jumps up and grabs the white chalk.

7   "Watch this, Tatsu," she says to me. Mario steps aside as Katie begins in the middle of a square. The square fills with white as the chalk gets smaller and smaller.

8   Finally, she stands. "A snow bank," she announces.

9   Fujio, Mario, and I cheer and clap. "Bravo! Bravo!"

10   Katie sits back down on the steps and leans back. I can tell she and the boys are thinking cool thoughts. I get up and make a big black "X" across my hot sun picture. Then, I go and sit right in the middle of Katie's snow bank. It's so cool it doesn't even melt.

Vocabulary Skills

Listen to the sound of the **c** in *cool*. Circle the words below that have the same sound as the **c** in *cool*.

1. cover   cereal

2. chin   corner

3. center   coming

4. cell   clap

When a short word has an **ing** ending, the syllable break comes between the word and its ending. So, *cooling* divides into *cool / ing*. For each word below, draw a line to divide the word into syllables.

5. b u i l d i n g

6. d r a w i n g

7. b e i n g

Reading Skills

1. Why do Mario and Katie choose to draw pictures of cool water and a snow bank?

   _____

   _____

2. Why does Tatsu cross out her own picture of the sun?

   _____

   _____

3. Do you think that thinking about cool things can help a person cool down? Write why or why not.

   _____

   _____

4. Can you remember a hot day? How did it feel? What did you do to cool down?

   _____

   _____

   _____

Study Skills

Two sets of guide words from a dictionary are shown here in bold print. Beside each entry word below, write the page number on which it would be found.

chalk / check   p. 194
chew / chore   p. 201

1. chime _____

2. chief _____

3. chapter _____

4. chive _____

5. cheap _____

6. chatter _____

7. charm _____

8. chimney _____

Drawings on the Wall

What might you have been doing if you lived 17,000 years ago?

1 The year, if anyone were counting, is around 15,000 B.C. You are probably looking for food, maybe using an animal skin to carry water, and possibly tending a fire to keep warm. Oh, and there's one other thing. You might have been drawing pictures on the walls of your cave.

2 We don't know why you drew the pictures. You had to go deep into the cave to do it, so you must have had a plan. You probably took a lamp made out of animal fat with you. Some of us think you drew pictures to bring good luck when you hunted. Others think the spears in some of the pictures mean that you were teaching other people to hunt.

3 For paint, you mixed animal fat with various things, such as dirt or berries. You used the ragged end of a stick to brush or dab the paint onto the wall. Sometimes, you didn't feel like using any color and you used the end of a stick that had been burned in the fire. It made broad black marks, much like modern artists make with chalk.

4 You drew what you saw around you—animals such as buffalo, deer, horses, and sometimes birds and fish. You drew people, but not very often. Sometimes, you made handprints or basic shape patterns on the wall.

5 You'll be happy to know that we think your pictures are really quite good. The buffalo look strong and powerful. And many of the horses and deer look graceful. You drew their shapes well.

6 We have found your drawings in more than 130 caves, mostly in France and England. We wonder if there are more that we haven't found yet. We wonder so many things, but we'll just have to satisfy ourselves with admiring your drawings. We're glad you made them.

Vocabulary Skills

Circle the correct letters to complete each word. Write the letters in the blank.

1. The stick burned in the f_____e.

   ar   er   ir

2. Did you know you were an _____tist?

   er   ar   ir

3. We think the pict_____es are quite well done.

   ir   or   ur

4. We adm_____e them very much.

   ir   ur   er

A **suffix** is a group of letters added to the end of a word that changes the meaning of the word. The suffix **-ful** means "full of." So, *joyful* means "full of joy."

Add **ful** to the words below. Use the new words to complete the sentences.

power	grace	care

5. The artists paid _____ attention to details.

6. The curving necks of the horses look very _____.

7. The great size of one buffalo makes it look especially _____.

Write a compound word using the underlined words in each sentence.

8. Some artists made <u>prints</u> of a <u>hand</u> on the wall.

   _____

9. Did you <u>brush</u> the <u>paint</u> on with a stick?

   _____

Reading Skills

1. This article is mostly about

   _____ animals that lived thousands of years ago.

   _____ early cave art.

   _____ how early people survived.

2. What did early cave artists use for paint?

   _____

3. Where did early artists make their drawings?

   _____

4. Early cave art has been found in more than _____ caves.

5. How do you like the cave art shown on this page? How is it the same or different from other drawings you have seen of mammoths?

   _____

   _____

Roman Wall Art

Read to see what Romans put on their walls.

1   Do you have pictures all over the walls of your home? If you don't, maybe you would like to. How about a scene from an old, famous story? Or maybe you would like a picture of a famous world leader having a meeting with other important people.

2   If you had lived in Rome about 2,000 years ago, you could have had a picture like these on a wall in your home. I don't mean just "on" a wall. I mean the whole wall could have been the picture.

3   Romans would often create sculptures on the sides of their buildings, near the top. These sculptures, called **bas-relief**, would be raised out of the flat exterior wall. This would create the illusion of the sculptures coming out of the background.

4   An artwork that covers a wall is a **mural**. *Mural* comes from *murus*, the Latin word for "wall." That seems fitting because the Romans (who spoke Latin) were great muralists. Some of their murals showed characters from Rome's many **myths**, or traditional stories. Other scenes showed important historical events. And others showed common events. One mural that still exists shows a bakery. In front, customers wait in line. The baker stands behind a counter, and behind him are bakery supplies. The mural gives us much information about the Rome of 2,000 years ago.

5   Sometimes, instead of painting a mural, Romans used an art form called **mosaic**. A mosaic is a picture formed by tiles, or tiny pieces of glass or pottery. The pieces are arranged, then held in place with glue or something similar to cement. One Roman mosaic is so large that it is made up of about a million tiny tiles. The size of this mosaic tells us that the person who owned the home was either very important, very wealthy, or both.

6   What if murals for our homes were still popular? What pictures do you suppose would be on the walls at your house? And what might people 2,000 years from now learn about your family and your world from those pictures?

Vocabulary Skills

Form the plural of each word below by changing the **y** to **i** and adding **es**. Write the word on the line.

1. supply _____

2. story _____

3. family _____

4. bakery _____

Form a contraction from each pair of words. Write the contraction on the line.

5. do not _____

6. will not _____

7. can not _____

8. did not _____

Reading Skills

1. Would you like to have a mural in your home? Write why or why not.

_____

_____

_____

2. Do you think the author wrote this article to make you laugh, give you information, or persuade you to do something?

_____

3. The author included some bold words in the article. She wanted readers to learn those words, so she included their meanings nearby. Find one of the words and look for its meaning. Write the word and its meaning here.

_____

_____

Write the best word to complete each sentence below.

4. I would like a _____ of a garden on my wall. (jacket, picture, notebook)

5. The bread in the Roman _____ mural looks yummy. (bakery, crown, sticky)

6. Would you like to use a million tiny _____ to make a mosaic? (pieces, motions, signs)

Study Skills

Number each list of words below in alphabetical order.

1. _____ story   2. _____ ago

_____ picture   _____ home

_____ world   _____ whole

_____ scene   _____ wall

From Lucy

What does Lucy share with her pen pal?

Dear Isabel,

1   First, I have to say that I just love your name. When my teacher was assigning pen pals, I hoped I would get you, and I did. I'm glad our teachers were pen pals when they were younger, because now we get to be pen pals.

me

2   I am Lucy. My name is really Lucinda, but no one ever calls me that. I am the only person in the whole third grade with red hair. I pretend that I don't like it, but secretly I don't mind. It sets me apart from the crowd. Mom says it's easy to spot me in the third-grade choir.

3   I have a mother, a father, and a little brother. My dad plans houses for people. Sometimes he works at his office, and sometimes he works at home. Mom takes care of us. She also paints things, like flower pots and little signs for people's gardens, and sells them. My little brother plays with trucks. That's pretty much all he does.

4   The neatest thing we did this summer was go to the beach. It was my first trip to the ocean. We drove all day from West Virginia to South Carolina and stayed in a hotel not too far from the beach. I loved the sand! We walked all along the shore and found pretty stones and little sea creatures that I had never seen before. I'll never forget the sound of the waves as they rolled and rolled into the beach.

5   Do you realize that it's possible that you and I have touched the same water? My teacher says that currents in the ocean keep it moving all the time. Maybe the water on the beach in South Carolina had come from the Dominican Republic.

6   I know that's kind of a goofy idea, but it helps me to think that we're not very far away from each other. I hope you can write back soon. I am eager to hear all about you and your family.

Your pen pal,
Lucy

Vocabulary Skills

Use the words below to complete the sentences. You will use each word twice.

pen	spot

1. Please use a _____, not a pencil.

2. It's easy to _____ her; she's the only one with red hair.

3. Please put the dogs in their _____.

4. Oh, the ink made a _____ on my paper.

In each row below, circle the three words that belong together.

5. letter postcard desk stamp

6. brother mother aunt teacher

7. sky sand stones rocks

8. beach grass hill mountain

Add the ending **-ly** to each word. Use the new words to complete the sentences. If the base word ends in a consonant followed by **y**, change the **y** to **i**, then add **ly**.

eager	secret	easy

9. Lucy _____ thought of many things to say to Isabel.

10. She waits _____ for Isabel's letter.

11. Don't tell anyone that Lucy _____ doesn't mind her red hair.

Reading Skills

1. The members of Lucy's family are

_____

_____.

2. What is Lucy's real name?

_____

3. Where does Lucy's pen pal live? How do you know?

_____

_____

_____

4. What details do we learn about Lucy from her letter?

_____

_____

_____

5. What do you think will happen after Lucy finishes writing her letter?

_____

_____

At the Shore

Read to see what's at the beach and why.

The Beach

1   When you close your eyes and imagine a beach, what do you see? Do you see steep cliffs and rocks washed by waves? Or do you see a long strip of gleaming sand, with waves gently lapping at the edges? Both pictures are correct. It just depends where on Earth you are standing.

2   In addition to sandy beaches and rocky beaches, many other beaches are covered with gravel or stones that would be unpleasant or difficult to walk on. One thing is common among beaches, though. They all have some kind of rock or stone material. Why?

3   It starts with the constant motion of water against a shore. Soil and plant material get washed away. Then, add wind, rain, and frost, which all work with the water to break down solid rock into smaller pieces. The temperature, the strength of the waves, and the type of rock all affect how quickly, or slowly, the rock breaks down.

The Waves

4   Now what about those waves? If you've been to the shore, you've seen them. They can nibble at your toes in the sand, or they can be loud and crashing and dangerous. You can blame the wind.

5   When the wind blows over the ocean or even a lake, it "gives" some of its energy to the water. The water, in turn, moves. The hard part to understand is that a wave does not move forward across the surface. The water in a wave moves up and down. Think of how a rug acts when you shake it. A wave appears to roll along the surface of the rug, but any point on that rug moves only up and down, not forward.

6   The next time you are on a beach, think about all these processes—the water and wind, the rain and frost. Without them, there would be no beach.

Vocabulary Skills

Write the words from the article that have these meanings.

1. sloping sharply

   _____
   Par. 1

2. always present; happening again and again

   _____
   Par. 3

3. the uppermost part of a thing

   _____
   Par. 5

When something happened in the past, add **ed** to the action word. Some words, however, do not follow that pattern.

Use each word pair to complete a sentence.

| shake—shook |
| grow—grew |
| find—found |

4. I will _____ many shells today. Yesterday, I _____ many also.

5. Does seaweed _____ in the water? Jan told me it _____ on the beach.

6. You can _____ this shell, but I _____ it already and didn't hear anything.

Reading Skills

1. What do beaches have in common?

   _____

   _____

2. Why do beaches have stones or sand on them?

   _____

   _____

3. What causes waves?

   _____

4. Why does the article mention a rug?

   _____

   _____

Study Skills

1. This article has two sections. What are they titled?

   _____

   _____

2. If you were especially interested in water, what section would you look under?

   _____

From Isabel

What does Isabel write in reply to her pen pal's letter?

Dear Lucy,

1   I think Lucinda is very pretty. But Lucy seems very friendly, so I will stay with Lucy. I loved getting your letter. I never knew anyone with red hair before.

2   I am Isabel. You already know that, I guess. I have long black hair. My mother says it looks green when the sun shines on it. I think she is just kidding, though.

3   You are so lucky to have a little brother. I have four sisters! They are all older than I am, and they all think they can tell me what to do. If I had a younger brother (or sister), I would never be bossy.

4   Maybe our fathers should work together! Your father plans houses, and my father builds houses. Maybe they should build one in South Carolina, and we could meet there. What do you think?

5   My mama takes care of us, too. She is the best cook in the world. Papa always says that it's good he has to work for a living. Otherwise, he would sit around and eat all day!

6   I am glad you like the beach. Here on my island, it would be a sad thing if someone didn't like the beach. Sometimes, when Papa comes home early from work, we take picnics to the beach. If we stay after dark, Papa plays his guitar. Those are the best days. The next time you see the moon, think of me and Mama dancing on the beach in its light.

Your pen pal,
Isabel

Vocabulary Skills

Match each word in the first list with its antonym in the second list. Write the letter in the blank.

1. _____ younger   **a.** short
2. _____ before   **b.** older
3. _____ long   **c.** worst
4. _____ best   **d.** after

Add **'s** at the end of a word to show that something belongs to someone. Then, write the name in the correct blank.

Isabel	Mama	Papa

5. _____ cooking is the best.
6. Isabel loves to hear _____ guitar.
7. Lucy will like _____ letter.

Reading Skills

Isabel wrote a friendly letter to her pen pal. She began the letter with "Dear Lucy." That is the **greeting**. She ended her letter with "Your pen pal, Isabel." That is the **closing** of the letter.

1. Suppose you are writing a letter. Write the greeting of your letter here. Remember to put a comma after your greeting.

   _____

2. Now write the closing of your letter. Note that there is a comma between the closing words and your name.

   _____

Write **T** if the sentence is true. Write **F** if the sentence is false.

3. _____ Isabel is the oldest child in her family.
4. _____ Isabel's father makes his living by playing guitar.
5. _____ Isabel thinks her mother is a good cook.
6. _____ Isabel sometimes feels bossed around by her sisters.

Study Skills

Use the table of contents below to answer the questions.

Dominican Republic
Table of Contents

1. Land 3
2. People 9
3. Government 15
4. Industry 23
5. Culture 27

1. How many chapters are in this book? _____

2. On what page does the chapter about government begin? _____

3. If you wanted to learn about the island's rivers, in what chapter should you look? _____

The Dominican Republic

Read to find out about this small island nation.

Where Is It?

1   South of Florida, a string of islands dots the ocean. One of them is Hispaniola (*hiss pan YO la*). Its name points to the fact that Christopher Columbus visited the island in 1492. As a result, Spain ruled the island for the next 300 years. Two nations now share the island. Haiti makes up the western third. The Dominican Republic makes up the eastern two-thirds.

How Big Is It?

2   The Dominican Republic's area is about 18,000 square miles. That's about the same size as Connecticut and Rhode Island combined. The island's population of 8 million, however, is about twice the population of those two states.

What Happens There?

3   Most people live close to the island's coast. Most of the cities are there, and so is the best farmland. Sugar cane has been the island's most important crop for hundreds of years. The mountainous interior is split by deep valleys where farmers raise cattle.

What Is There to Do?

4   Like many other tropical islands, the Dominican Republic views tourism as an important industry. The coastal cities, especially, depend on tourists to fill their hotels and restaurants. The natural beauty of the beaches and of the forest regions draw Dominicans and tourists alike.

5   When you're ready for something else, wander into town to see local craftspeople and artists and their wares. If you like parades and costumes, go in February for Carnival. Music, dancing, and people in colorful masks will greet you at nearly every street corner. Whether you go to join the crowds or get away from the crowds, there will be a place for you in the Dominican Republic.

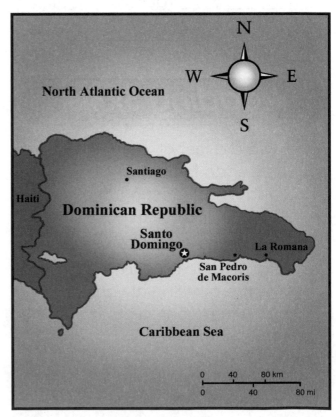

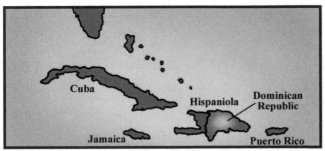

Vocabulary Skills

Say *below*. Notice the sound that the letters **ow** make. Circle the words below that have the same sound as **ow** in *below*.

1. shower   coastal   howl   count

2. mountain   about   know   pool

3. grow   towel   tower   brook

4. troop   sound   crown   toast

The suffix **-ous** means "full of." So, *gracious* means "full of grace." Write the meanings of these words.

5. mountainous _____

6. joyous _____

7. wondrous _____

Reading Skills

Find information in the article to complete the chart. (Determine the population of Connecticut and Rhode Island based on other information in the article.)

Dominican Republic	Connecticut and Rhode Island
1. Area: _____	Area: _____
2. Population: _____	Population: _____

3. What does the article say about the Dominican Republic's weather?

_____

4. What do you know about the weather in Connecticut and Rhode Island? How would it compare to the Dominican Republic's weather?

_____

_____

_____

Study Skills

1. If the author wanted to add this sentence to the article, under what heading should it go?

Workers also harvest valuable lumber from the coastal forests.

_____

2. If you need a quick reminder about the location of the island, under what heading should you look?

_____

Look at the map to answer these questions.

3. Which city is the capital? How can you tell?

_____

4. What city is farther north than the others?

_____

Lucy and Isabel: Pen Pals

How are Lucy and her pen pal the same and different?

1 "Mom! I just got a letter from my pen pal," called Lucy when her mom walked in the door.

2 Mrs. Teeman smiled. "Oh, good! Maybe you won't have to camp out beside the mailbox any more," she teased Lucy. "Tell me all about it while we unpack the groceries."

3 "Okay," said Lucy, pulling fruit out of a bag. "We have a lot in common. She likes to go to the beach, too. Can you imagine dancing under the stars?" Lucy twirled around with a bunch of bananas for a partner.

4 Mrs. Teeman laughed at Lucy's excitement. "Hmm, sounds nice. What else does she say?" she asked.

5 "Oh, our dads are both in the house-building business," Lucy chattered on. "Isabel thinks they should build a house in South Carolina. Then, we could meet at the beach for vacation."

6 "Sounds like a dreamy vacation," commented Mrs. Teeman from inside the refrigerator.

7 Lucy paused thoughtfully over a box of spaghetti. "Of course, we're different in some ways, too."

8 "Well, that's natural," Mrs. Teeman assured Lucy. "In what ways?"

9 "The biggest difference is that Isabel has four older sisters." Lucy made a face as she went on. "She says she wants a little brother or sister."

10 "Did you tell her about having a little brother?" asked Mrs. Teeman.

11 Lucy nodded and said, "Isabel says she would never be bossy."

12 "That sounds like a good plan," said Mrs. Teeman, with a motherly glance.

13 "And," continued Lucy, "she says her mother is a great cook."

14 Mrs. Teeman looked crushed. "That's different from your life?"

15 Lucy realized that what she had said hadn't come out quite right. "Oh," she said quickly, "that's one of the ways Isabel and I are the same." Lucy gave her mother a quick hug and made a hasty exit. "I better go answer Isabel's letter."

Vocabulary Skills

Write the words from the story that have these meanings.

1. to take the contents out of something

   _____
   Par. 2

2. belonging to or shared by two people

   _____
   Par. 3

3. talked quickly and informally

   _____
   Par. 5

4. stopped briefly

   _____
   Par. 7

The words below are broken into syllables. Sound out each syllable. Then, write the word and say it to yourself as you write.

5. re/frig/er/a/tor _____

6. spa/ghet/ti _____

7. i/mag/ine _____

8. moth/er/ly _____

Reading Skills

1. Lucy is excited because _____

   _____.

2. Lucy's mother is just returning from

   _____.

3. Does Lucy seem helpful or selfish in this story? Give reasons for your answer.

   _____

   _____

Lucy notices that she and her pen pal, Isabel, are alike in some ways and different in others. Help her compare. Write what is the same about both girls in the space provided. Then, write what is different about each girl.

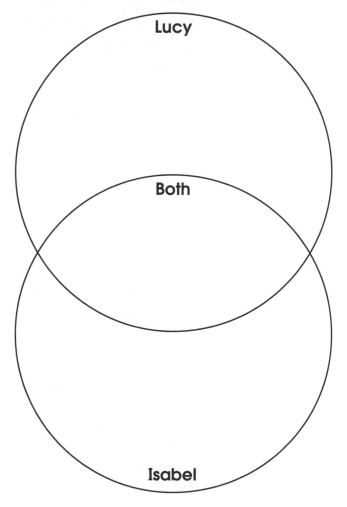

Lucy

Both

Isabel

Phone Troubles

What happens when Kyle doesn't pay attention to a telephone message?

1   Somebody called for Mom. It was somebody from school. I didn't really catch the name. I said my mom was mowing the lawn, and so the lady asked if I could take a message. I said, "Sure."

2   Then, she started talking about cakes and Thursday after school and I said sure, cakes were great. I was trying to get my math homework done because Rick was waiting for me next door. Then, the lady said something about the principal and I said, "Sure, I know," because everyone knows the principal. Finally, she stopped talking and said, "Okay?"

3   I said, "Okay." Then, I remembered to say, "Thank you for calling," just like Mom taught me. Then, I hung up, finished my math, and headed for Rick's house.

4   I didn't remember the call until the next morning at breakfast. "Oh, you had a call yesterday while you were out mowing the lawn, Mom."

5   "Oh? Who was it, Kyle?" she said, between toast bites.

6   Uhhh. Think, think. "It was about Thursday after school," I said, announcing the only detail I could remember.

7   "What about it?" Mom's getting a little prickly. I better handle this well.

8   "There's a bake sale. The principal was asking for stuff." I felt good about remembering the principal.

9   Well, to make a long story short, it was the president of the PTO who called. Mom says she's very important. She was asking if mom could bake a cake for the principal because they were going to surprise him for his birthday.

10   Mom shows up on Thursday after school with a little plate of cookies, thinking there's a bake sale. Mrs. Essman looks at her like she's from Mars and asks where the cake is. Of course, Mom doesn't know anything about a cake or a birthday or anything. Now, I'm in the doghouse, and my brother and I have to learn telephone manners from Mom.

Vocabulary Skills

Choose a synonym from the box to replace the underlined word. Write that synonym on the line.

called	crawl	raced

1. "Mom! Phone call for you!" I <u>said</u> out the door.

    _____

2. When I finished my homework, I <u>went</u> to Rick's house.

    _____

3. I was so tired I could hardly <u>get</u> up the stairs.

    _____

Listen to the sound of **th** in *thin*. Circle the words below that have the same sound as the **th** in *thin*. The sound may be at the beginning, middle, or end of a word.

4. then   think

5. mother   math

6. thank   them

7. Thursday   they

Make a check next to the meaning that fits the underlined word in each sentence.

8. Kyle <u>felt</u> good about remembering the phone call.

    _____ past form of *feel*

    _____ a fabric, usually made from wool

9. I thought I handled the telephone message pretty <u>well</u>.

    _____ a hole with water in it

    _____ in a good way

Reading Skills

1. Number the sentences to show the order in which things happened.

    _____ Kyle gives Mom the phone message.

    _____ Mom goes to school on Thursday.

    _____ Mom goes out to mow the lawn.

    _____ Kyle takes a phone call for Mom.

    _____ Mrs. Essman asks Mom where the cake is.

2. Why does Mom take cookies to school on Thursday?

    _____

    _____

Phone Manners

What telephone manners does Mom teach her sons?

1 "Now, repeat after me. When we answer the phone, we say: 'Hello. Reese residence. This is so-and-so speaking.'"

2 My brother and I repeated after Mom in slow, droning tones, "Hello. Reese residence. This is Kyle-thony speaking." We each said our names in the "so-and-so" spot, so Kyle and Anthony came out *Kyle-thony*. I thought about giggling, but the look on Mom's face told me not to.

3 "That's very good." Mom was talking to us as if we were four-year-olds. "Now," she continued, "if the person on the other end of the phone says 'May I speak to your mother?', what do you say? Kyle?" I knew this one.

4 I recited just like Mom had taught us. "Yes, you may. May I ask who is calling, please?"

5 "That's very good," said Mom in her sing-songy teacher voice. "Okay, you seem to have the basics. Let's talk about taking phone messages." She shot me a look. I had goofed up on one little phone message the other day. That's why my brother and I were in the Phone Manners from Mom class. "What are the three basic parts of a phone message?"

6 Anthony and I recited: "Name. Number. Write it down."

7 "Very good," sang Mom. "Oh, and there's actually a fourth part. Can anyone figure out what it is?" She looked right at me. I couldn't think.

8 "Deliver the message," Mom answered her own question, "on the same day the call comes in." I smiled weakly. That was a small detail that I had overlooked the other day, along with name, number, and writing it down.

9 "Any questions?" Mom asked brightly. Anthony raised his hand. "Yes?"

10 "Will there be a test?"

11 "Every time the phone rings," said Mom, quite seriously. "Class dismissed."

Vocabulary Skills

Write the words from the story that have these meanings.

1. happened or done again and again

   _____
   Par. 2

2. gave knowledge or skill to someone

   _____
   Par. 4

3. failed to notice or do something

   _____
   Par. 8

Circle the correct letters to complete each word. Write the letters in the blank.

4. What did you say to the p_____son on the phone?

   ar   er   ir

5. What are the three basic p_____ts of a phone message?

   ar   ur   ir

6. I hope I pass the Phone Mann_____s from Mom class.

   ur   ir   er

Reading Skills

1. What important parts of a phone message did Kyle forget the other day?

   _____

   _____

2. Look at the illustration. What do you think Mom is saying? Write the dialogue.

   _____

   _____

Study Skills

You have just attended the Phone Manners from Mom class. How should you respond to these telephone situations?

1. The phone rings. You answer it by saying, "_____

   _____."

2. Your dad is reading a book on the porch. The phone rings and the person says "May I speak to your father?" What do you say?

   _____

   _____

3. Your mom is washing her hair and can't come to the phone. What are the four important parts of a phone message?

   _____

   _____

Number the list of words below in alphabetical order.

4. _____ telephone

   _____ repeat

   _____ tones

   _____ speaking

Hold the Phone!

What do the boys notice about Uncle Dale?

1 Kyle hung up the phone and tore the top sheet off the message pad. He posted it in the middle of the refrigerator door with his favorite magnet. Ever since Mom's Phone Manners class, he had followed the rules: Get the name. Get the number. Write it down. Deliver it.

2 As Kyle positioned the polar bear, his uncle Dale walked into the kitchen. "Hey, Uncle Dale. What's up?"

3 "Oh, not much," shrugged Uncle Dale. "Your mom invited me over for supper." Uncle Dale often dropped by just in time for a meal.

4 "Oh, cool," said Kyle, on his way out the door with Anthony. Just then the phone rang. Uncle Dale answered it.

5 "Yeah?" he said. Kyle and Anthony froze. Their mom had taught them not to say "yeah" on the phone. She said it was bad manners. They wondered how Uncle Dale had missed that lesson. "Yeah." Uncle Dale said again and nodded. "Yeah, okay." Silence. "Sure." He hung up.

6 After a moment, Anthony was too curious not to ask. "Who was that?"

7 "It was for your mom," said Uncle Dale, paging through a magazine. Kyle and Anthony looked at each other.

8 "Um, there's a message pad here," offered Kyle, "if you want to write a message down."

9 Uncle Dale looked up for a moment. "Oh, it's okay. I'll remember. It was someone from school about a meeting."

10 "What meeting?" asked Mom, peeling off her garden gloves at the kitchen door. Uncle Dale looked up.

11 "Oh, hi, Sis. Ahh, there's a meeting … on Saturday morning." Uncle Dale's face suddenly looked a little pained.

12 "Where? What about?" asked Mom. Kyle and Anthony gritted their teeth.

13 "Oh, you know, one of those school meetings," said Uncle Dale slowly. "It starts at 9:30...I think."

14 Mom made a face. She looked at her sons. All three of them turned to Uncle Dale and recited: "Get the name! Get the number! Write it down! Deliver it!"

Vocabulary Skills

Abbreviations may be used to save time or space. Replace each underlined item in the message below with an abbreviation from the box.

a.m.	p.m.
Fri.	Wed.
Mon.	

Dr. Shafer's office called—555-4116—to reschedule your check-up. It could be <u>Wednesday</u> at 2 in the <u>afternoon</u>, or it could be <u>Friday</u> at 10:30 in the <u>morning</u>. Please let them know by <u>Monday</u> at 5:00.

1. Wednesday _____
2. afternoon _____
3. Friday _____
4. morning _____
5. Monday _____

Say these words aloud: *silence, polar*. Notice the long vowel sound at the beginning of the words. When dividing these words into syllables, break them after that long vowel: *si / lence, po / lar*.

Now say these words aloud: *copy, lemon*. Notice the short vowel sound at the beginning. When dividing these

words into syllables, the middle consonant stays with that first short vowel: *cop / y, lem / on*.

Divide these words into syllables. They all follow the rules stated above.

6. c l o s e t
7. m o m e n t
8. o k a y
9. c a b i n
10. o v e r

Reading Skills

1. What surprised Kyle and Anthony about Uncle Dale's phone conversation?

_____ the fact that he had even answered the phone

_____ the way he spoke

_____ the length of the conversation

2. Number the sentences to show the order in which events happened.

_____ Uncle Dale gets a lesson on how to take phone messages.

_____ Uncle Dale arrives.

_____ Uncle Dale answers the phone.

_____ Kyle takes a phone message.

_____ Mom enters the kitchen.

_____ Kyle greets Uncle Dale.

Telephones: How Do They Work?

Read to find out how telephones work.

1   We're going to take a little trip. We're going to travel with your voice as it leaves your mouth, goes through a telephone, moves through the telephone network, and arrives at your friend's telephone.

2   Let's say you already dialed the telephone. A computer instantly connected you to your friend's telephone, based on the numbers you pressed. The sound waves made by your voice enter the microphone in your telephone. The sound waves then travel by wire. With the help of an electric power supply, an electric current runs along the wire. Your sound waves disrupt that flow of electricity. When the current is flowing smoothly, your friend hears no sound. When your sound waves have affected the flow, the varying electrical current reaches the speaker in the earpiece of your friend's telephone. A device there changes the electrical currents back into sound waves. The sound waves enter your friend's ear, and your conversation has begun.

3   As technology goes, telephones are thought to be quite simple. People knew almost 400 years ago that sound waves could travel along a wire. Then, in 1875, Alexander Graham Bell invented a telephone that could be put to practical use. Imagine what he would think if he could see his fellow Americans on the telephone today.

Vocabulary Skills

In each row below, circle the three words that belong together.

1. wave   talk   laugh   sing

2. pal   buddy   pest   friend

3. electricity   hearing   current   wire

Form the plural of each word below by adding **s**. Write the word on the line.

4. voice _____

5. telephone _____

6. network _____

7. computer _____

8. wave _____

9. wire _____

Reading Skills

1. The article says it's not your voice, but _____ made by your voice, that enter the telephone's microphone.

2. When the current in a telephone wire is flowing smoothly, what does the person on the other end hear?

_____

3. When sound waves interrupt the flow of current, what does the person on the other end hear?

_____

4. How long ago did people know that sound could travel along a wire?

_____

5. How long ago did Alexander Graham Bell invent the telephone?

_____

Write **F** next to each sentence that is a fact. Write **O** next to each sentence that is an opinion.

6. _____ Sound waves travel along a wire with the help of electrical current.

7. _____ The telephone is the most important invention of the last 200 years.

8. _____ Without the telephone, modern businesses would fail.

9. How do you and other members of your family use the telephone today?

_____

_____

10. What would it be like if you had to get along without telephones? How else would you communicate?

_____

_____

_____

Honey to the Rescue

What happens when there is no syrup for the pancakes?

1   *What's that smell?* I snuggled under the covers. I was still too close to sleep to identify it. It was a good smell, but it wasn't a normal smell. *What day is it? Saturday? What's that smell?*

2   My brain finally jerked me awake as I began to put the pieces together. Saturday. That smell…pancakes! I grabbed my fuzzy robe and rushed down the stairs. Mom stood at the griddle, humming and flipping pancakes. Without a word, I slid into my spot.

3   Dad nodded at me. He was spooning mushed up baby food from a jar into my little brother's mouth. Poor kid. He was too young to eat pancakes. My little sister sat at the table, fork in hand, quiet for once, waiting for her pancakes.

4   Mom turned away from the griddle with the first plateful of pancakes. I smiled charmingly at her; she smiled back. Two for Dad, two for Lisa, two for me. *Excellent.* I spread some butter, then reached for the syrup. *Nope, no syrup.* I went to the refrigerator and opened the door. I looked in the usual spots. I looked again: on the door shelves, behind the milk jug, behind the orange juice. Panic rose. I turned and scanned the kitchen counter. *Nope, no syrup.*

5   "Mom?" I asked calmly. "Where's the syrup?"

6   She kept flipping. "Isn't it there in the door? Or behind the milk?"

7   "No. I looked twice." But I looked again, just to make sure. Then, Mom looked.

8   "Oh, don't tell me we're out. I was sure we had some," she moaned.

9   Dad paused his spooning. "I can run to the store, I guess."

10   "Oh, wait," interrupted Mom. She stepped up onto a stool and reached up to the top shelf in the cupboard. Out came a plastic bear. "Honey to the rescue!" she announced. "Gramps sent this last summer. I keep forgetting about it."

11   She plunked the bear down on the table and went back to the griddle. *Well, there's no syrup, so there's no choice.* I swirled some of the bear's golden goop onto my pancakes. I tasted. I chewed. I smiled. *Honey to the rescue, indeed.*

Vocabulary Skills

Write the words from the story that have these meanings.

1. got comfortable

    _____
    Par. 1

2. usual

    _____
    Par. 1

3. singing with lips closed

    _____
    Par. 2

4. container, usually made of glass

    _____
    Par. 3

5. to coat something with a layer of something

    _____
    Par. 4

These pairs of words sound the same, but have different meanings and spellings. Write the correct word from each pair to complete each sentence.

heard—herd	sea—see
bare—bear	scent—sent

6. The honey _____ was full.

7. The heavy _____ of flowers brought the bees.

8. She couldn't _____ the syrup in the fridge.

9. Lisa groaned when she _____ there was no syrup.

Reading Skills

1. What clues tell you that the narrator is in bed? Write the words or phrases from the story.

    _____

    _____

2. How do you know that having pancakes for breakfast must be a special thing?

    _____

    _____

3. The word that best describes this family is

    _____ rough.

    _____ noisy.

    _____ pleasant.

Circle the name or word that each underlined word, or **pronoun**, stands for.

4. Mom said she was sure there was still some syrup.

    Lisa   syrup   Mom

5. When he heard the news, Dad offered to go to the store.

    store   Dad   news

6. Lisa waited quietly. She loved pancakes most of all.

    Mom   Lisa   pancakes

Honey

What are the author's opinions about honey?

1 Honey lasts pretty much forever. That's one reason why it should be our national food. Did you know they found honey in one of the pyramids? It wasn't moldy or rotten. They tasted it, and it still tasted like honey. It didn't taste like 3,000-year-old honey, it just tasted like honey. Those Egyptian bees must have been something else.

2 Honey is sweet. That's another reason it should be our national food. Americans love sweet things. I happen to like sweet things, and honey is at the top of my list. I use honey to sweeten my tea and my breakfast cereal. I put it on bread and toast. I use it instead of part of the sugar when I bake certain cookies and breads. Have you had a honey-glazed ham lately? Yum!

3 I think the bees would like it if we made honey our national food. People would plant special gardens. The bees could gather nectar everywhere.

Nectar is sort of like sugar water. Flowers produce it to attract bees and butterflies. While gathering nectar, the creatures just happen to get pollen on them, which they take to the next flower. The flowers would not survive without this mixing of pollen. Then, bees mix a special substance called an *enzyme* with the nectar. To avoid a long explanation, let's just say it changes the nectar into a special kind of sugar that we call *honey*.

4 Bees don't just make honey, they eat it, too. Or, rather, they feed it to young bees, called *larvae*, in the hive. Honey also is used to keep the bees' food from spoiling. Bees store pollen in cells within the hive. Each cell is then sealed with honey to prevent bacteria from entering.

5 See how useful honey is? Even if it's not our national food, stop and admire a honey bee some day, and remember to say thank you. Then, go have some bread and honey.

Vocabulary Skills

Words whose meanings are opposite are called **antonyms**. Match each word in the first list with its antonym in the second list. Write the letter in the blank.

1. _____ old   **a.** sour

2. _____ light   **b.** young

3. _____ sweet   **c.** fresh

4. _____ spoiled   **d.** heavy

Form a contraction from each pair of words. Write the contraction on the line.

5. that is _____

6. was not _____

7. did not _____

8. let us _____

9. do not _____

10. it is _____

Reading Skills

1. List the reasons the author gives for making honey our national food.

_____

_____

_____

_____

2. Do you think those are good reasons for naming honey as a national food? Write why or why not.

_____

_____

_____

3. Sometimes, an author has more than one purpose for writing. What two purposes do you think this author had for writing the honey article?

_____ to entertain readers

_____ to give an explanation of honey bees' lives

_____ to persuade readers that honey is good

_____ to describe how honey resists bacteria

4. This article is mostly about

_____ how good honey is.

_____ the food value of honey.

Write the best word to complete each sentence below.

5. It's amazing that the honey didn't _____. (burst, spoil, mend)

6. I like to _____ honey on hot toast. (spread, clap, handle)

7. As bees _____ nectar, they also spread pollen. (collect, enter, change)

A Sad Song

Read to see why people sing songs.

1   "....Then mend it, dear Georgie, dear Georgie, dear Georgie. Then mend it, dear Georgie. Dear Georgie, mend it."

2   Eliza raised her hand. Mr. Hamlin, the music teacher, had been watching her. She hadn't been singing. "Eliza?"

3   Eliza looked puzzled. "I understand why people would want to make a song about someone named Liza...." Eliza began. Several classmates turned around and made good-natured faces at her. "But why would anyone want to make a song about a dumb bucket with a hole in it?" A burst of giggling came from the class.

4   "Hmm, well that's a good question," answered Mr. Hamlin. "Would anyone like to guess?"

5   "You told us it was an old song, so I suppose people would have used buckets a lot." Natalie offered.

6   "That's right," encouraged Mr. Hamlin. "A bucket would have been a very common thing." Mr. Hamlin let them think some more. Then, he went on. "Remember last week when we worked on 'Down by the Well'? What did we say about that song?"

7   Jansen remembered. "We said that going to the well to get water was something people did every day."

8   "So," cut in Eliza, "they made up songs about stuff they did every day?"

9   Mr. Hamlin gave a big nod. "People sang songs when they were happy or sad, when they worked, or when they rested. Songs helped people express their feelings."

10   "I guess that's not much different from us," said Eliza, still thinking it over. "I sang a sad song just this morning."

11   "Oh? What about?" said Mr. Hamlin.

12   Eliza sang her answer. "*There's a hole in my sock, dear Mommy, dear Mommy....*"

Vocabulary Skills

Add **ed** to an action word to show that something happened in the past. If the base word ends in a silent **e**, add only **d**.

Add **d** or **ed** to each word. Use the new words to complete the sentences.

turn	offer	raise
name	watch	

1. Eliza wasn't singing, so Mr. Hamlin had _____ her.

2. When she spoke, some students _____ around and smiled.

3. Eliza thought the song was _____ after her.

4. As the song ended, Eliza _____ her hand.

5. Natalie was the only one who _____ an idea.

Some action words do not follow the usual pattern. Instead of adding **-ed** to show that something happened in the past, change the entire word.

Match each action word with its past form.

6. _____ give   a. sang
7. _____ think   b. drew
8. _____ draw   c. made
9. _____ sing   d. thought
10. _____ make   e. gave

Listen to the sound of **g** in *Georgie*. Circle the words below that have the same sound as the **g** in *Georgie*. The sound may be at the beginning, middle, or end of a word.

11. energy   giggle
12. good   giant
13. guess   change
14. engine   again

Reading Skills

1. Write **R** next to two sentences that tell about real things.

_____ Anyone can make up a song.

_____ A song can be happy or sad.

_____ The words of a song are always true.

Study Skills

In what volume of the encyclopedia would you look to find these topics? Write the volume number.

1. songs _____   2. music _____
3. violins _____   4. harps _____
5. drums _____   6. flutes _____

What Is Folk Music?

Do you know any folk songs?

1   Wouldn't you like to know how people used to live, what they did, and how they felt about things? Sing a folk song, and maybe you'll find out!

2   Though people are still writing folk music, most of the songs we think of as folk songs are old. They come from America's earliest settlements, from war battlefields, and from pioneers' log cabins. And, of course, some of the songs' roots go even farther back to the settlers' original countries.

3   We don't know who wrote most folk music. What we do know we learn from the words of the songs. They tell about everyday life, soldiers lost in wars, and hard work. The words tell us that people's feelings haven't changed much over the last few hundred years.

4   Within the body of folk music are two types of songs. Ballads are longer songs that usually relate a story. They may be serious or funny. Folk songs are shorter songs that might relate a feeling or an experience a person had.

5   Folk music covers endless topics and countless emotions. Coming up with an average folk song or ballad is almost impossible because there is so much variety. Here, however, is the first verse of "Farewell, Nancy." In it, a sailor expresses both sadness and hope. These feelings, if anything, are common to many folk songs.

Farewell, my dearest Nancy,

Since I must now leave you;

Unto the salt seas

I am bound for to go;

But let my long absence

Be no trouble to you,

For I shall return

In the spring, as you know.

Vocabulary Skills

Say *flow*. Notice the sound that the letters **ow** make. Circle the words below that have the same sound as **ow** in *flow*. The sound may come at the beginning, middle, or end of the word.

1. bound   you   course   tow

2. country   trouble   throat   vowel

3. around   two   know   countless

4. now   sound   voice   follow

Use the following words to form compound words. Then, use the compound words to complete the sentences.

battle	every
day	field

5. It was very sad to visit the
_____.

6. Some folk songs recall the
_____ tasks that people
used to do.

Reading Skills

1. What is the difference between a
ballad and a folk song?

_____

_____

_____

2. Why do you suppose someone
wrote "Farewell, Nancy"?

_____

_____

3. Why do you think someone
would make a song about saying
good-bye?

_____

_____

_____

4. "When Johnny Comes Marching
Home Again" is a well-known
ballad. Even if you don't know the
words, the title hints at the song's
story. What do you think it is?

_____

_____

_____

Study Skills

Number each list of words below in
alphabetical order.

1. _____ settlers   2. _____ wrote

_____ folk   _____ war

_____ music   _____ write

_____ songs   _____ words

Peanut Butter Plus

Read to see what the boys learn about their grandpa.

1 "Thicker, please," requested Max. His grandmother looked at him with a raised eyebrow.

2 Max shrugged. "I really like it."

3 "All right," sighed Grandma, "a little more, but then that's enough, I think."

4 "Thanks, Grandma," smiled Max. Grandma, Max, and A.J. were putting together a picnic. They were going to take it to the far field to check on Grandpa, who was planting corn.

5 "May I have one just like that?" asked A.J. "Please?" Grandma just laughed and shook her head.

6 "I never have seen anyone who likes peanut butter as much as you two do," she said, shaking her head.

7 The boys grinned. It was true. They loved peanut butter. A peanut butter and jelly sandwich for lunch every day made them perfectly happy.

8 Grandma went on. "Of course, it was your grandpa who invented the best peanut butter sandwich ever."

9 The boys had never heard this story. They threw questions at her. "How? When? What is it?"

10 Grandma looked out the window, as if the story were out there. "It was when we were first married. Your grandpa had broken his leg and couldn't do any farm work. So I was out on the tractor. The hay had to be brought in, after all. Grandpa had never really cooked, but he felt as if he should have a meal ready when I came in from the field. So he put together a peanut butter-bacon-banana sandwich on toast. I thought it looked awful, but I didn't want to hurt his feelings. So I took a bite." Grandma stopped, dreaming out the window.

11 The boys couldn't wait. "And?"

12 A little smile curved at Grandma's lips. "It was delicious."

Vocabulary Skills

Circle the word that is a synonym of the underlined word or words in each sentence.

1. Grandpa had a meal <u>ready</u> when Grandma came in from the field.

   extra   silent   prepared

2. The boys did not want to <u>alter</u> their lunch habits.

   change   refresh   outlive

3. Grandpa's farm called for a lot of hard <u>work</u>.

   attempt   mistrust   labor

Add **'s** at the end of a word to show that something belongs to someone. Add **'s** to each name. Then, write the name in the correct blank.

| A.J. | Grandpa | Max |

4. _____ sandwich was delicious.

5. Max washed his brother _____ apple.

6. Grandma added peanut butter to _____ sandwich.

Circle the correct letters to complete each word. Write the letters in the blank.

7. Grandma and Grandpa are f_____mers.

   er   ar   ir

8. Grandma had to drive the tract_____.

   ar   or   er

9. Grandma's lips c_____ved in a little smile.

   er   ir   ur

Reading Skills

1. What do Grandma and Grandpa do for a living?

   _____

2. Do you think Grandma likes peanut butter? Why?

   _____

   _____

3. How do you like the sound of a peanut butter-bacon-banana sandwich?

   _____

   _____

   _____

4. What do you think will happen next?

   _____

   _____

   _____

Working for Peanuts

Who is responsible for the popularity of peanuts?

1   What can you do with nuts? A scientist named George Washington Carver answered that question, over and over again. We owe thanks to him for more than 300 products.

2   When Carver was born in 1864, he was a slave on a farm in Missouri. Later, as a teenager and a freedman, he worked on a farm and managed to put himself through high school. At age 30, he became the first black student at his college in Iowa. In 1896, he became the first black teacher to be hired at another college in Iowa. Several years later, he took a job at a college in Alabama, where he worked until his death in 1943.

3   Carver studied agriculture, the science of farming. His research made huge improvements in farming in the southern United States. In particular, Carver studied peanuts. He knew that the South could not grow only cotton. Planting cotton year after year wore out the soil and made it useless. Carver learned that if farmers planted cotton one year and peanuts the next, the soil remained healthy.

4   To encourage this practice, Carver came up with new uses for the peanut. Would you like to try peanut and prune ice cream? How about lotion or shampoo made from peanuts? Perhaps you would prefer to make paint from peanuts, or maybe you would like to bake with peanut flour. Glue? Paper? Rubber? The list goes on and on. He also came up with similar uses for pecans and other nuts.

5   Carver did not profit from most of his inventions. He didn't feel that it was right to sell his ideas. Rather, he gave them freely to help farmers and fellow scientists. Carver's life is one that we could all use as an example.

Vocabulary Skills

Write the words from the article that have these meanings.

1. between the ages of 13 and 19

   _____
   Par. 2

2. given a job

   _____
   Par. 2

3. serious study

   _____
   Par. 3

4. changes or additions that make something better

   _____
   Par. 3

5. make money

   _____
   Par. 5

Form a contraction from each pair of words. Write the contraction on the line.

6. there is _____

7. did not _____

8. he would _____

9. who will _____

10. they are _____

The words below are broken into syllables. Sound out each syllable. Then, write the word and say it to yourself as you write.

11. ag/ri/cul/ture _____

12. im/prove/ments _____

13. in/ven/tions _____

14. sci/en/tists _____

Reading Skills

1. This article is mostly about

   _____ Carver's work with peanuts.

   _____ Carver's fame as a scientist.

   _____ Carver's fight to get an education.

2. George Washington Carver lived from _____ until _____.

3. While in college, he studied

   _____,

   which is the study of

   _____.

4. Carver made hundreds of products from peanuts. List some that the article mentions.

   _____

   _____

5. Which of the products seems the most interesting or the most unusual to you? Write why.

   _____

   _____

Write **F** next to each sentence that is a fact. Write **O** next to each sentence that is an opinion.

6. _____ Carver saved Southern farmers from ruining the land.

7. _____ Planting peanuts after cotton keeps the soil healthy.

8. _____ Carver is America's greatest black scientist.

All Wrapped Up

What kind of wrapping paper do Stephanie and her mom use?

1 "Do you really think he'll like it?" I asked Mom for the fiftieth time. She gave me the same answer every time.

2 "Of course he will, Steph, and mostly because you made it."

3 I wasn't completely sure about her answer. I wanted him to like his Father's Day present because it was great, not just because I made it. Dad had been talking about building a birdhouse all winter. He just hadn't had time. So, I asked Mom to help me make one. One wall was a little crooked, but other than that it looked pretty good, I thought.

4 We had nailed the roof on after school. Now, we were hunting in the attic for a box to put the birdhouse in.

5 "Is this one big enough?" I asked, holding up an old shoe box.

6 "Mmm, I don't think the roof would quite fit. Here's one. What do you think?" asked Mom.

7 "Looks good. I'm sure that'll be big enough. Let's go wrap it." Father's Day was two days away, but I was eager to have my present all ready.

8 "Okay. I have a great idea for wrapping paper," said Mom. She loved to drop hints.

9 "Oh, did you buy some new stuff?" I asked.

10 "Nope," said Mom simply.

11 "Uhhh, well, what's the idea, then?" You just never knew with my mom.

12 Mom spread out a big sheet of plain light brown paper. There were already some paints sitting on the counter, along with some sponges and rubber stamps. Mom waved her arms over the collection. "We're going to print our own wrapping paper. Won't that make your present extra special?"

13 Well, I thought my present was already extra special, but if it made Mom happy, I guess I would do it. "Okay. Extra special paper for an extra special present. Let's do it."

NAME

Vocabulary Skills

These pairs of words sound the same, but have different meanings. Write the correct word from each pair to complete each sentence.

| rap—wrap | two—too |
| wood—would | great—grate |

1. I wonder if you _____ reach the paint for me.

2. We have only _____ rubber stamps to use.

3. If you need me, just _____ on my office door.

4. That noise is really starting to _____ on my nerves.

Say *because* aloud. Notice the long vowel sound at the beginning of the word. When dividing this word into syllables, break it after the long vowel: *be / cause*.

Now, say *present*, which means "a gift." Notice the short vowel sound at the beginning. When dividing this word into syllables, the middle consonant stays with the first short vowel: *pres / ent*.

Divide these words into syllables. They all follow the rules stated above.

5. o t h e r   8. p a p e r

6. e n o u g h   9. n e v e r

7. e a g e r

Reading Skills

Write the best word to complete each sentence below.

1. Stephanie and her mom look for a box in the _____. (attic, entrance, ending)

2. Stephanie was proud that she had _____ her present. (waved, built, filled)

3. Stephanie was _____ about Mom's wrapping idea. (clever, crazy, curious)

Circle the name or word that each underlined word, or **pronoun**, stands for.

4. Mom said <u>she</u> had an idea for wrapping paper.

   idea   Mom   Stephanie

5. When <u>she</u> heard the idea, Stephanie was doubtful.

   idea   Mom   Stephanie

6. Mom was all ready. <u>She</u> had already set out the supplies.

   supplies Mom   Stephanie

Study Skills

Number the group of words below in alphabetical order.

1. _____ answer   _____ present

   _____ birdhouse _____ great

Making Prints

Read to see how to create your own prints.

[1] Making prints is easy and fun, and there is no limit to the designs you can make.

Supplies

paints (tempera or acrylic)

paintbrushes

stamps* (see note below)

sheets of tissue or craft paper

plastic lids

newspaper

* Use store-bought rubber or sponge stamps. Or make your own stamps, using household materials such as fruits or vegetables, kitchen utensils, bottle caps, office supplies, and so on.

Instructions

1. Cover your work area with newspaper.

2. Pour small amounts of paint into plastic lids (so you can easily dip your stamps into the paint).

3. Lay out a sheet of paper. Imagine the design you are going to print.

4. Dip a stamp into some paint. If you want to use more than one color for a stamp, apply paint to areas of the stamp with a paintbrush.

5. Press the stamp, paint side down, firmly on the paper without jiggling or sliding the stamp from side to side.

6. Hold the paper down with one hand while you lift the stamp.

7. Repeat steps 4, 5, and 6 until your design is complete.

8. Let paper dry. To clean up, wash stamps and paintbrushes in warm, soapy water.

[2] In addition to making wrapping paper, you can use this same process to decorate boxes, book covers, or even walls and furniture (with permission, of course). Use your imagination and print away!

Vocabulary Skills

Form the plural of each word below by adding **s**, **es**, or by changing **y** to **i** and adding **es**. Write the word on the line.

1. design _____

2. supply _____

3. paintbrush _____

4. stamp _____

5. box _____

The prefix **multi-** means "many" or "much." The prefix **micro-** means "small" or "short." Combine one of these prefixes with each word in the box. Then, use the new words to complete the sentences.

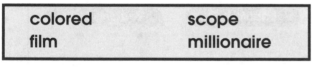

| colored | scope |
| film | millionaire |

6. I looked at old newspapers at the library on the _____ machine.

7. My design will be bright and _____.

8. This fossil is so small you need a _____ to see it.

9. I'll start a stamp printing company and become a _____.

Reading Skills

1. The author used a numbered list for the instructions. Why do you think this was done?

_____

_____

_____

2. What other kinds of instructions, with numbered lists, have you seen?

_____

_____

3. Number the sentences to show the order in which to complete the stamping project.

_____ Dip stamp into paint.

_____ Press stamp on paper.

_____ Put paint in plastic lids.

_____ Let dry.

_____ Lay out sheet of paper.

_____ Lift the stamp.

4. Why do the instructions say you should put small amounts of paint in plastic lids?

_____

5. What can you think of that you would like to decorate with stamps?

_____

_____

_____

Answer Key

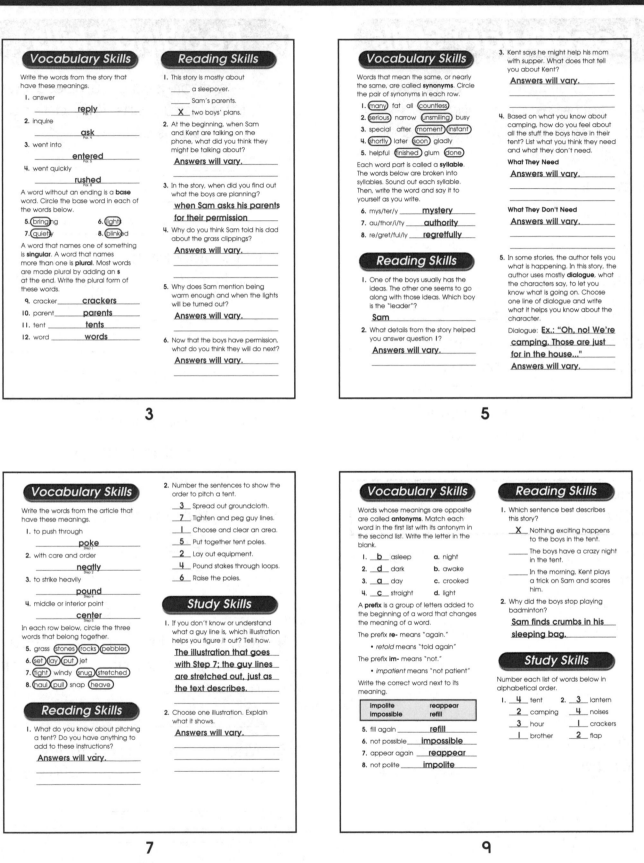

Page 3

Vocabulary Skills

Write the words from the story that have these meanings.

1. answer
   reply _Par. 1_
2. inquire
   ask _Par. 4_
3. went into
   entered _Par. 5_
4. went quickly
   rushed _Par. 8_

A word without an ending is a **base** word. Circle the base word in each of the words below.

5. (bring)ing   6. (light)
7. (quiet)ly   8. (blink)ed

A word that names one of something is **singular**. A word that names more than one is **plural**. Most words are made plural by adding an **s** at the end. Write the plural form of these words.

9. cracker   **crackers**
10. parent   **parents**
11. tent   **tents**
12. word   **words**

Reading Skills

1. This story is mostly about
   _____ a sleepover.
   _____ Sam's parents.
   X two boys' plans.

2. At the beginning, when Sam and Kent are talking on the phone, what did you think they might be talking about?
   Answers will vary.

3. In the story, when did you find out what the boys are planning?
   when Sam asks his parents
   for their permission

4. Why do you think Sam told his dad about the grass clippings?
   Answers will vary.

5. Why does Sam mention being warm enough and when the lights will be turned out?
   Answers will vary.

6. Now that the boys have permission, what do you think they will do next?
   Answers will vary.

Page 5

Vocabulary Skills

Words that mean the same, or nearly the same, are called **synonyms**. Circle the pair of synonyms in each row.

1. (many) fat all (countless)
2. (serious) narrow (unsmiling) busy
3. special after (moment) (instant)
4. (shortly) later (soon) gladly
5. helpful (finished) glum (done)

Each word part is called a **syllable**. The words below are broken into syllables. Sound out each syllable. Then, write the word and say it to yourself as you write.

6. mys/ter/y   **mystery**
7. au/thor/i/ty **authority**
8. re/gret/ful/ly **regretfully**

Reading Skills

1. One of the boys usually has the ideas. The other one seems to go along with those ideas. Which boy is the "leader"?
   Sam

2. What details from the story helped you answer question 1?
   Answers will vary.

3. Kent says he might help his mom with supper. What does that tell you about Kent?
   Answers will vary.

4. Based on what you know about camping, how do you feel about all the stuff the boys have in their tent? List what you think they need and what they don't need.

   What They Need
   Answers will vary.

   What They Don't Need
   Answers will vary.

5. In some stories, the author tells you what is happening. In this story, the author uses mostly **dialogue**, what the characters say, to let you know what is going on. Choose one line of dialogue and write what it helps you know about the character.

   Dialogue: **Ex.: "Oh, no! We're**
   camping. Those are just
   for in the house..."
   Answers will vary.

Page 7

Vocabulary Skills

Write the words from the article that have these meanings.

1. to push through
   poke _Step 1_
2. with care and order
   neatly _Step 2_
3. to strike heavily
   pound _Step 4_
4. middle or interior point
   center _Step 5_

In each row below, circle the three words that belong together.

5. grass (stones) (rocks) (pebbles)
6. (set) (lay) (put) jet
7. (tight) windy (snug) (stretched)
8. (haul) (pull) snap (heave)

Reading Skills

1. What do you know about pitching a tent? Do you have anything to add to these instructions?
   Answers will vary.

2. Number the sentences to show the order to pitch a tent.
   3 Spread out groundcloth.
   7 Tighten and peg guy lines.
   1 Choose and clear an area.
   5 Put together tent poles.
   2 Lay out equipment.
   4 Pound stakes through loops.
   6 Raise the poles.

Study Skills

1. If you don't know or understand what a guy line is, which illustration helps you figure it out? Tell how.
   The illustration that goes
   with Step 7; the guy lines
   are stretched out, just as
   the text describes.

2. Choose one illustration. Explain what it shows.
   Answers will vary.

Page 9

Vocabulary Skills

Words whose meanings are opposite are called **antonyms**. Match each word in the first list with its antonym in the second list. Write the letter in the blank.

1. **b** asleep   a. night
2. **d** dark   b. awake
3. **a** day   c. crooked
4. **c** straight   d. light

A **prefix** is a group of letters added to the beginning of a word that changes the meaning of a word.

The prefix **re-** means "again."
  • *retold* means "told again"

The prefix **im-** means "not."
  • *impatient* means "not patient"

Write the correct word next to its meaning.

| impolite | reappear |
| impossible | refill |

5. fill again   **refill**
6. not possible   **impossible**
7. appear again   **reappear**
8. not polite   **impolite**

Reading Skills

1. Which sentence best describes this story?
   X Nothing exciting happens to the boys in the tent.
   _____ The boys have a crazy night in the tent.
   _____ In the morning, Kent plays a trick on Sam and scares him.

2. Why did the boys stop playing badminton?
   Sam finds crumbs in his
   sleeping bag.

Study Skills

Number each list of words below in alphabetical order.

1. **4** tent   2. **3** lantern
   2 camping   **4** noises
   3 hour   **1** crackers
   1 brother   **2** flap

Answer Key

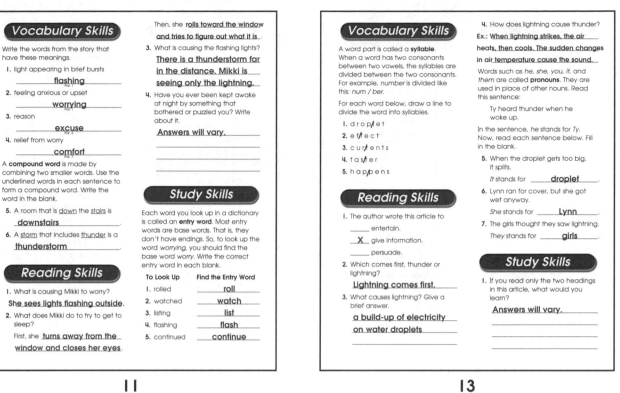

Vocabulary Skills

Write the words from the story that have these meanings.

1. light appearing in brief bursts
   flashing
   Par. 1
2. feeling anxious or upset
   worrying
   Par. 1
3. reason
   excuse
   Par. 6
4. relief from worry
   comfort
   Par. 7

A **compound word** is made by combining two smaller words. Use the underlined words in each sentence to form a compound word. Write the word in the blank.

5. A room that is <u>down</u> the <u>stairs</u> is
   downstairs
6. A <u>storm</u> that includes <u>thunder</u> is a
   thunderstorm

Reading Skills

1. What is causing Mikki to worry?
   She sees lights flashing outside.
2. What does Mikki do to try to get to sleep?
   First, she **turns away from the window and closes her eyes.**

Then, she **rolls toward the window and tries to figure out what it is**.

3. What is causing the flashing lights?
   There is a thunderstorm far in the distance. Mikki is seeing only the lightning.
4. Have you ever been kept awake at night by something that bothered or puzzled you? Write about it.
   Answers will vary.

Study Skills

Each word you look up in a dictionary is called an **entry word**. Most entry words are base words. That is, they don't have endings. So, to look up the word *worrying*, you should find the base word *worry*. Write the correct entry word in each blank.

To Look Up	Find the Entry Word
1. rolled	**roll**
2. watched	**watch**
3. listing	**list**
4. flashing	**flash**
5. continued	**continue**

11

Vocabulary Skills

A word part is called a **syllable**. When a word has two consonants between two vowels, the syllables are divided between the two consonants. For example, *number* is divided like this: *num / ber*.

For each word below, draw a line to divide the word into syllables.

1. d r o p / l e t
2. e f / f e c t
3. c u r / r e n t s
4. f a s / t e r
5. h a p / p e n s

Reading Skills

1. The author wrote this article to
   ___ entertain.
   X give information.
   ___ persuade.
2. Which comes first, thunder or lightning?
   Lightning comes first.
3. What causes lightning? Give a brief answer.
   a build-up of electricity on water droplets

4. How does lightning cause thunder?
   Ex.: **When lightning strikes, the air heats, then cools. The sudden changes in air temperature cause the sound.**

Words such as *he, she, you, it,* and *them* are called **pronouns**. They are used in place of other nouns. Read this sentence:

   Ty heard thunder when he woke up.

In the sentence, *he* stands for Ty. Now, read each sentence below. Fill in the blank.

5. When the droplet gets too big, it splits.
   It stands for **droplet**.
6. Lynn ran for cover, but she got wet anyway.
   She stands for **Lynn**.
7. The girls thought they saw lightning.
   They stands for **girls**.

Study Skills

1. If you read only the two headings in this article, what would you learn?
   Answers will vary.

13

Vocabulary Skills

Homophones are words that sound alike but have different spellings and different meanings. Complete each sentence below by writing the correct word in the blank.

1. Smokey the **Bear** is easy to recognize. (Bare, Bear)
2. The **wood** in our forests is valuable. (wood, would)

Homographs are words that are spelled the same but have different meanings. For example, *bat* can name a stick used in baseball or a flying mammal. Choose the correct word below to complete each pair of sentences.

park	ships

3. The **ships** were lined up in the harbor.
   Grandma always **ships** a package for my birthday.
4. I looked for a place to **park** the car.
   We had a picnic in the **park**.

Reading Skills

Put a check next to the sentences that are true.

1. **✓** The idea for Smokey the Bear started in the 1940s.
2. ___ Smokey the Bear lives in New Mexico.
3. ___ The Forest Service made posters in honor of a bear cub that died in a fire.
4. **✓** Smokey the Bear was a drawing first, then a real bear.

Write M next to the sentences that tell about make-believe things.

5. ___ Smokey the Bear lived in a zoo for many years.
6. **M** Smokey the Bear speaks to campers about the danger of forest fires.
7. **M** Smokey the Bear used to help firefighters put out fires.
8. Why was Smokey the Bear created? Write the phrase or sentence from the article that tells you.
   To protect America's forests

15

Vocabulary Skills

Circle the correct letters to complete each word. Write the letters in the blank.

1. The pots were behind the flow **er** shop.
   ir   (er)   ur
2. Rosa planted a g **ar** den in the pots.
   (ar)   or   er
3. She sat on the f **ir** e escape and watched the plants grow.
   ur   (ir)   er
4. Rosa dashed up the stairs to her ap **ar** tment.
   er   (ar)   ir

The missing words in these sentences contain the letters ee or ea. Fill in the blanks.

5. Rosa waited for **three** days before she asked about the pots.
6. She fell asleep and **dreamed** about her garden.
7. It didn't matter that the pots were **cheap** and plastic.
8. Rosa planted **seeds** in her pots.

Reading Skills

A **fact** is something that can be proven true. An **opinion** is what someone thinks or feels. Check the sentences that are facts.

1. **✓** Vegetables can be grown in pots.
2. ___ Creating a garden on a fire escape is difficult.
3. ___ Any garden is beautiful.
4. **✓** Plants need soil and water.
5. Number the sentences to show the order in which things happened.
   3 Rosa bought potting soil.
   2 Rosa took the pots home.
   4 Rosa planted her seeds.
   1 Rosa saw the pots.
6. Check the words or phrases that best describe Rosa.
   ___ selfish
   ___ tends to waste time
   ✓ likes the outdoors
   ✓ appreciates beauty

17

Answer Key

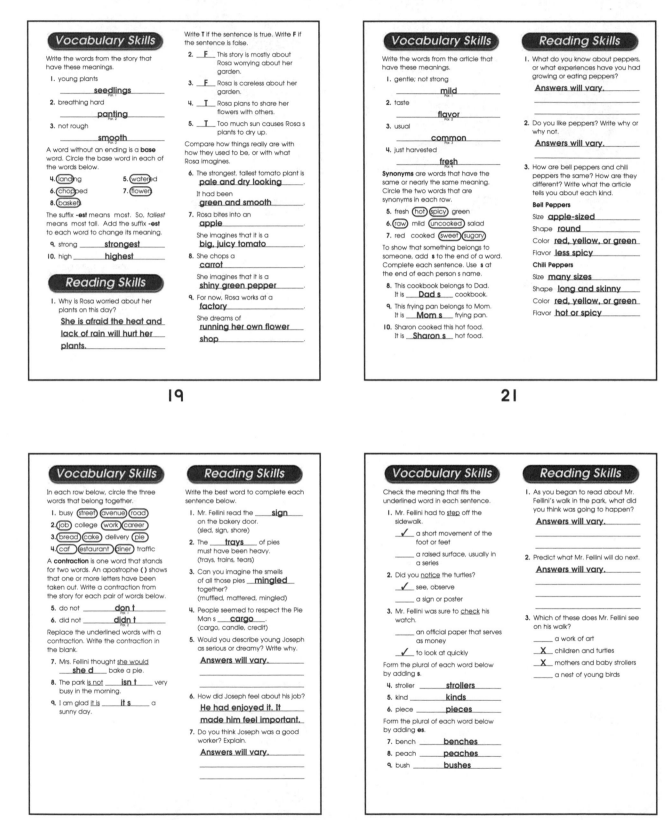

Page 19

Vocabulary Skills

Write the words from the story that have these meanings.

1. young plants

   seedlings Par. 1

2. breathing hard

   panting Par. 2

3. not rough

   smooth Par. 2

A word without an ending is a **base** word. Circle the base word in each of the words below.

4. (land)ing   5. (water)ed

6. (chopp)ed   7. (flower)s

8. (basket)s

The suffix **-est** means most. So, *tallest* means most tall. Add the suffix **-est** to each word to change its meaning.

9. strong _____ **strongest**

10. high _____ **highest**

Reading Skills

1. Why is Rosa worried about her plants on this day?

   She is afraid the heat and lack of rain will hurt her plants.

Write **T** if the sentence is true. Write **F** if the sentence is false.

2. __F__ This story is mostly about Rosa worrying about her garden.

3. __F__ Rosa is careless about her garden.

4. __T__ Rosa plans to share her flowers with others.

5. __T__ Too much sun causes Rosa's plants to dry up.

Compare how things really are with how they used to be, or with what Rosa imagines.

6. The strongest, tallest tomato plant is **pale and dry looking** .

   It had been **green and smooth** .

7. Rosa bites into an **apple** .

   She imagines that it is a **big, juicy tomato** .

8. She chops a **carrot** .

   She imagines that it is a **shiny green pepper** .

9. For now, Rosa works at a **factory** .

   She dreams of **running her own flower shop** .

Page 21

Vocabulary Skills

Write the words from the article that have these meanings.

1. gentle; not strong

   mild Par. 1

2. taste

   flavor Par. 2

3. usual

   common Par. 3

4. just harvested

   fresh Par. 4

Synonyms are words that have the same or nearly the same meaning. Circle the two words that are synonyms in each row.

5. fresh (hot) (spicy) green

6. (raw) mild (uncooked) salad

7. red   cooked (sweet) (sugary)

To show that something belongs to someone, add **s** to the end of a word. Complete each sentence. Use **s** at the end of each person's name.

8. This cookbook belongs to Dad.
   It is **Dad s** cookbook.

9. This frying pan belongs to Mom.
   It is **Mom s** frying pan.

10. Sharon cooked this hot food.
    It is **Sharon s** hot food.

Reading Skills

1. What do you know about peppers, or what experiences have you had growing or eating peppers?

   Answers will vary.

2. Do you like peppers? Write why or why not.

   Answers will vary.

3. How are bell peppers and chili peppers the same? How are they different? Write what the article tells you about each kind.

   Bell Peppers

   Size **apple-sized**

   Shape **round**

   Color **red, yellow, or green**

   Flavor **less spicy**

   Chili Peppers

   Size **many sizes**

   Shape **long and skinny**

   Color **red, yellow, or green**

   Flavor **hot or spicy**

Page 23

Vocabulary Skills

In each row below, circle the three words that belong together.

1. busy (street) (avenue) (road)

2. (job) college (work) (career)

3. (bread) (cake) delivery (pie)

4. (caf) (restaurant) (diner) traffic

A **contraction** is one word that stands for two words. An apostrophe ( ) shows that one or more letters have been taken out. Write a contraction from the story for each pair of words below.

5. do not _____ **don t** Par. 1

6. did not _____ **didn t** Par. 2

Replace the underlined words with a contraction. Write the contraction in the blank.

7. Mrs. Fellini thought she would bake a pie.
   she d

8. The park is not very busy in the morning.
   isn t

9. I am glad it is a sunny day.
   it s

Reading Skills

Write the best word to complete each sentence below.

1. Mr. Fellini read the _____ **sign** on the bakery door.
   (sled, sign, shore)

2. The _____ **trays** of pies must have been heavy.
   (trays, trains, tears)

3. Can you imagine the smells of all those pies _____ **mingled** together?
   (muffled, mattered, mingled)

4. People seemed to respect the Pie Man's _____ **cargo** .
   (cargo, candle, credit)

5. Would you describe young Joseph as serious or dreamy? Write why.

   Answers will vary.

6. How did Joseph feel about his job?

   He had enjoyed it. It made him feel important.

7. Do you think Joseph was a good worker? Explain.

   Answers will vary.

Page 25

Vocabulary Skills

Check the meaning that fits the underlined word in each sentence.

1. Mr. Fellini had to <u>step</u> off the sidewalk.

   ✓ a short movement of the foot or feet

   _____ a raised surface, usually in a series

2. Did you <u>notice</u> the turtles?

   ✓ see, observe

   _____ a sign or poster

3. Mr. Fellini was sure to <u>check</u> his watch.

   _____ an official paper that serves as money

   ✓ to look at quickly

Form the plural of each word below by adding **s**.

4. stroller _____ **strollers**

5. kind _____ **kinds**

6. piece _____ **pieces**

Form the plural of each word below by adding **es**.

7. bench _____ **benches**

8. peach _____ **peaches**

9. bush _____ **bushes**

Reading Skills

1. As you began to read about Mr. Fellini's walk in the park, what did you think was going to happen?

   Answers will vary.

2. Predict what Mr. Fellini will do next.

   Answers will vary.

3. Which of these does Mr. Fellini see on his walk?

   _____ a work of art

   __X__ children and turtles

   __X__ mothers and baby strollers

   _____ a nest of young birds

Answer Key

Page 27

Vocabulary Skills

Words whose meanings are opposite are called **antonyms**. Match each word in the first list with its antonym in the second list. Write the letter in the blank.

1. __a__ grow   a. shrink
2. __c__ city   b. tight
3. __d__ crowded   c. country
4. __b__ loose   d. empty

Listen to the beginning sound of *central*. Circle the words below that have the same sound as the *c* in *central*. (The sound may be at the beginning, middle, or end of the word.)

5. (cent)   crack
6. (fancy)   color
7. credit   (ceiling)
8. (pencil)   pinch

Each sentence below contains a compound word. Find the word. Write the two small words that make up the compound word.

9. The view from the top of the skyscraper was great!

__sky__ __scraper__

10. Mr. Fellini saw a goldfinch in a bush near the museum.

__gold__ __finch__

Reading Skills

1. The article contains a feature box titled "Central Park by the Numbers." What kind of information is in the box?

The box gives information about the size of the park and the number of things in it.

2. Why do you think this information was shown in a separate list instead of in the text?

Answers will vary.

3. When was Central Park planned?

__1858__

4. The park was a daring project because **the land was rocky, swampy, and muddy**

5. If you walked on all of the walking paths in the park, you would walk

58 miles

6. Which is greater, the number of trees or the number of benches?

the number of trees

27

Page 29

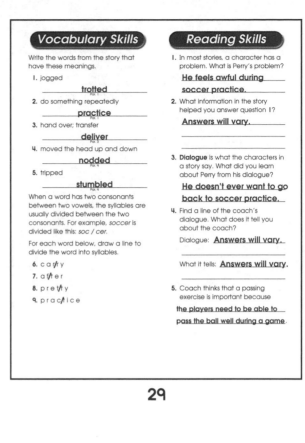

Vocabulary Skills

Write the words from the story that have these meanings.

1. jogged

__trotted__
Par. 1

2. do something repeatedly

__practice__
Par. 1

3. hand over; transfer

__deliver__
Par. 3

4. moved the head up and down

__nodded__
Par. 4

5. tripped

__stumbled__
Par. 4

When a word has two consonants between two vowels, the syllables are usually divided between the two consonants. For example, *soccer* is divided like this: *soc / cer*.

For each word below, draw a line to divide the word into syllables.

6. c a r/r y
7. a f/t e r
8. p r e t/t y
9. p r a c/t i c e

Reading Skills

1. In most stories, a character has a problem. What is Perry's problem?

He feels awful during soccer practice.

2. What information in the story helped you answer question 1?

Answers will vary.

3. **Dialogue** is what the characters in a story say. What did you learn about Perry from his dialogue?

He doesn't ever want to go back to soccer practice.

4. Find a line of the coach's dialogue. What does it tell you about the coach?

Dialogue: **Answers will vary.**

What it tells: **Answers will vary.**

5. Coach thinks that a passing exercise is important because

the players need to be able to pass the ball well during a game.

29

Page 31

Vocabulary Skills

Write the words from the story that have these meanings.

1. unable to say anything

__speechless__
Par. 9

2. unsteady; wobbly

__shaky__
Par. 10

3. be done

__finish__
Par. 12

To show that something happened in the past, add **ed** to a base word. Some words, however, do not follow normal spelling patterns. Read each sentence. Write the correct word in the blank.

ran	drove	shook

4. Today, I shake my head. Last week, I __shook__ my head.
5. Today, I run. Yesterday, I __ran__.
6. Today, you drive. Yesterday, you __drove__.

Complete each sentence below by writing the correct word in the blank.

7. This is the last __week__ of practice before school starts. (weak, week)

8. I thought we agreed to __meet__ at 10 o'clock. (meat, meet)

Reading Skills

1. Mrs. Rothman is speechless because **Perry has just said he wants to quit soccer**.

2. Check two words that tell how Perry probably felt.

  ✓ disappointed
  ___ proud
  ___ eager
  ✓ frightened

3. Perry says he wants to quit soccer because **he is weak; doesn't have what it takes**

4. Have you ever tried to do something that was hard, or that you had to work at? What was it?

Answers will vary.

Did you get discouraged? Did you quit?

Answers will vary.

5. Do you think Perry's decision is reasonable, or do you think he is giving up too easily? Explain.

Answers will vary.

31

Page 33

Vocabulary Skills

Circle the word that correctly completes each sentence. Write the word in the blank.

1. When you use __brown__ sugar, pack it into the measuring cup.

down   (brown)   crowd

2. Does it ask for stick cinnamon or __ground__ cinnamon?

sound   cloud   (ground)

3. I think the best part is the plump, juicy __raisins__.

chain   (raisins)   plain

Recipes often use short forms of words called **abbreviations**. Match the common recipe words in the box with their abbreviations.

cup	teaspoon
Fahrenheit	tablespoon

4. T. __tablespoon__
5. c. __cup__
6. F __Fahrenheit__
7. tsp. __teaspoon__

Recipes use many action words. Choose one of the action words in the box and write, in your own words, what you would do. Look back at the recipe for ideas.

stir	spread
mix	drizzle

Action word:
Answers will vary.

Reading Skills

Write these steps in the correct order. (Not all of the recipe's steps are here.)

• spread mixture into pan
• drizzle glaze
• grease the pan
• mix sugar, oil, and eggs
• remove from oven and cool

1. **grease the pan**
2. **mix sugar, oil, and eggs**
3. **spread mixture into pan**
4. **remove from oven and cool**
5. **drizzle glaze**

6. How long do the directions say to bake the bars?

16 to 22 minutes

7. The directions say to "drizzle honey glaze over bars." How did you know what honey glaze was?

Answers will vary.

33

Answer Key

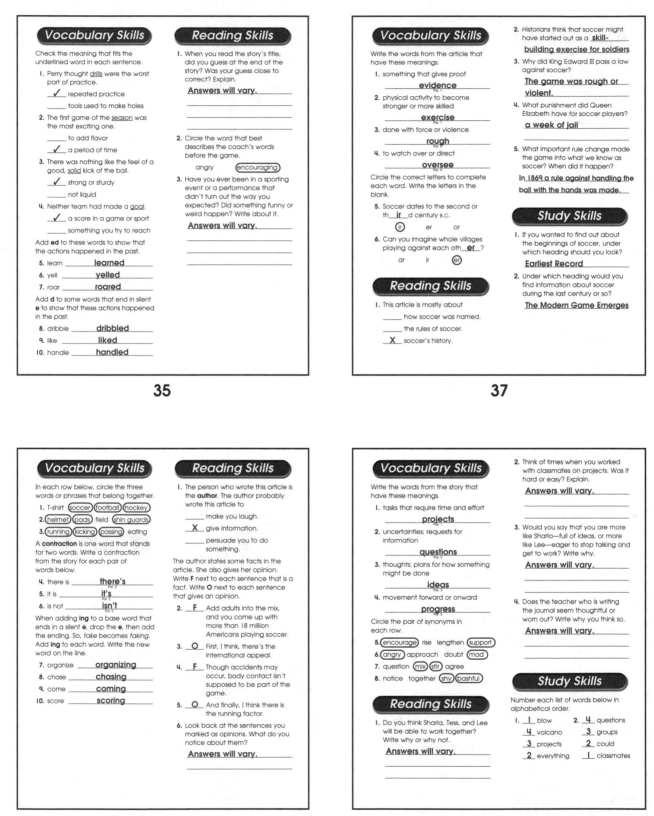

Page 35

Vocabulary Skills

Check the meaning that fits the underlined word in each sentence.

1. Perry thought drills were the worst part of practice.
   - ✓ repeated practice
   - _____ tools used to make holes

2. The first game of the season was the most exciting one.
   - _____ to add flavor
   - ✓ a period of time

3. There was nothing like the feel of a good, solid kick of the ball.
   - ✓ strong or sturdy
   - _____ not liquid

4. Neither team had made a goal.
   - ✓ a score in a game or sport
   - _____ something you try to reach

Add **ed** to these words to show that the actions happened in the past.

5. learn **learned**
6. yell **yelled**
7. roar **roared**

Add **d** to some words that end in silent **e** to show that these actions happened in the past.

8. dribble **dribbled**
9. like **liked**
10. handle **handled**

Reading Skills

1. When you read the story's title, did you guess at the end of the story? Was your guess close to correct? Explain.
   Answers will vary.

2. Circle the word that best describes the coach's words before the game.
   angry (encouraging)

3. Have you ever been in a sporting event or a performance that didn't turn out the way you expected? Did something funny or weird happen? Write about it.
   Answers will vary.

Page 37

Vocabulary Skills

Write the words from the article that have these meanings.

1. something that gives proof
   evidence
2. physical activity to become stronger or more skilled
   exercise
3. done with force or violence
   rough
4. to watch over or direct
   oversee

Circle the correct letters to complete each word. Write the letters in the blank.

5. Soccer dates to the second or th**ir**d century B.C.
   (ir)   er   or

6. Can you imagine whole villages playing against each oth**er**?
   ar   ir   (er)

Reading Skills

1. This article is mostly about
   - _____ how soccer was named.
   - _____ the rules of soccer.
   - X soccer's history.

2. Historians think that soccer might have started out as a **skill-building exercise for soldiers**.

3. Why did King Edward III pass a law against soccer?
   The game was rough or violent.

4. What punishment did Queen Elizabeth have for soccer players?
   a week of jail

5. What important rule change made the game into what we know as soccer? When did it happen?
   In 1869 a rule against handling the ball with the hands was made.

Study Skills

1. If you wanted to find out about the beginnings of soccer, under which heading should you look?
   Earliest Record

2. Under which heading would you find information about soccer during the last century or so?
   The Modern Game Emerges

Page 39

Vocabulary Skills

In each row below, circle the three words or phrases that belong together.

1. T-shirt (soccer) (football) (hockey)
2. (helmet) (pads) field (shin guards)
3. (running) (kicking) (passing) eating

A **contraction** is one word that stands for two words. Write a contraction from the story for each pair of words below.

4. there is **there's**
5. it is **it's**
6. is not **isn't**

When adding **ing** to a base word that ends in a silent **e**, drop the **e**, then add the ending. So, take becomes taking. Add **ing** to each word. Write the new word on the line.

7. organize **organizing**
8. chase **chasing**
9. come **coming**
10. score **scoring**

Reading Skills

1. The person who wrote this article is the **author**. The author probably wrote this article to
   - _____ make you laugh.
   - X give information.
   - _____ persuade you to do something.

The author states some facts in the article. She also gives her opinion. Write **F** next to each sentence that is a fact. Write **O** next to each sentence that gives an opinion.

2. F Add adults into the mix, and you come up with more than 18 million Americans playing soccer.
3. O First, I think, there's the international appeal.
4. F Though accidents may occur, body contact isn't supposed to be part of the game.
5. O And finally, I think there is the running factor.
6. Look back at the sentences you marked as opinions. What do you notice about them?
   Answers will vary.

Page 41

Vocabulary Skills

Write the words from the story that have these meanings.

1. tasks that require time and effort
   projects
2. uncertainties; requests for information
   questions
3. thoughts; plans for how something might be done
   ideas
4. movement forward or onward
   progress

Circle the pair of synonyms in each row.

5. (encourage) rise lengthen (support)
6. (angry) approach doubt (mad)
7. question (mix) (stir) agree
8. notice together (shy) (bashful)

Reading Skills

1. Do you think Sharla, Tess, and Lee will be able to work together? Write why or why not.
   Answers will vary.

2. Think of times when you worked with classmates on projects. Was it hard or easy? Explain.
   Answers will vary.

3. Would you say that you are more like Sharla—full of ideas, or more like Lee—eager to stop talking and get to work? Write why.
   Answers will vary.

4. Does the teacher who is writing the journal seem thoughtful or worn out? Write why you think so.
   Answers will vary.

Study Skills

Number each list of words below in alphabetical order.

1. 1 blow   2. 4 questions
   4 volcano   3 groups
   3 projects   2 could
   2 everything   1 classmates

Answer Key

Page 43

Vocabulary Skills

Write the words from the story that have these meanings.

1. a sticky substance

   __paste__

2. putting or placing somewhat carelessly

   __plopping__

A **compound word** is made by combining two smaller words. Find the compound word in each sentence. Write the two small words that make up the compound.

3. Tess was fussing about the paste and Lee didn't want to plan anything.

   __any__   __thing__

4. Well, the whole thing went downhill from there.

   __down__   __hill__

The prefix **un-** means "not." So, *unable* means "not able."

Read the words below. Write the correct word next to its meaning.

| unhappy | unfair | uncertain |

5. not certain   __uncertain__

6. not happy   __unhappy__

7. not fair   __unfair__

Reading Skills

This story is written in the form of a journal entry. The person who is writing uses *I* to refer to herself. She is the **narrator**, or the person telling the story.

1. Find a sentence that tells you that the narrator actually took part in the action of the story. Write the sentence here.

   __Answers will vary.__

2. The narrator, Sharla, disagreed with Lee about __whether to make the sides of the volcano smooth or rough__.

3. Sharla was upset because

   __she thought it was unfair to have to stay in at recess__

Each of the following sentences contains a pronoun. Write which word the pronoun stands for.

4. Lee didn't want to plan anything, she just wanted to jump in.

   She stands for   __Lee__

5. Tess can make the little village since she refuses to touch the volcano paste.

   She stands for   __Tess__.

43

Page 45

Vocabulary Skills

Complete each sentence below by writing the correct word in the blank.

1. We haven't completed __our__ project yet. (hour, our)

2. __Two__ of the girls could not agree. (To, Too, Two)

Some words look the same, but have different meanings. Choose the correct word below to complete the sentence. Then, write your own sentence using the word in a different way.

| well | can |

3. The water from the __well__ was cold.

   __Answers will vary.__

4. I don't see how Tess __can__ get away with it.

   __Answers will vary.__

Form the plural of each word below by adding **es**. Write the word on the line.

5. volcano   __volcanoes__

6. hero   __heroes__

7. potato   __potatoes__

8. echo   __echoes__

Reading Skills

1. In most stories, the characters have a problem. What problem do the characters in this story have?

   __They had disagreed about how to finish their project.__

2. What caused Mrs. Holt to call the girls up to her desk?

   __They weren't done with their project.__

3. What is Tess's idea?

   __X__ to show flowing lava

   _____ to make both sides smooth

   _____ to make the village larger

4. What is the result of Tess's idea?

   __The girls agree to make one side smooth and one side rough. Sharla and Lee can both get what they want.__

5. Where in the story do we learn that the teacher, Mrs. Holt, knows the girls are not getting along?

   __Where it says, "knowing perfectly well that there was a problem."__

45

Page 47

Vocabulary Skills

Write the words from the story that have these meanings.

1. feeling pleased and satisfied

   __proudly__

2. sends forth steam, lava, and ash

   __erupts__

3. to finish

   __complete__

4. to think the same; to have the same ideas

   __agree__

A word without an ending is a **base** word. Circle the base word in each of the words below.

5. (try)ing   6. (shape)d

7. (cover)ed   8. (girl)s

9. (please)d

Complete each sentence, using apostrophes correctly to show ownership.

10. This volcano belongs to the girls. It is the __girls'__ volcano.

11. The students had questions. The __students'__ questions were good ones.

12. The teachers went on vacation. The __teachers'__ vacations were well deserved.

Reading Skills

1. This story is mostly about

   _____ becoming best friends after working together.

   __X__ what the girls learned from their project.

   _____ how a teacher helped the girls get along.

2. How do the girls feel about their volcano project?

   __They are proud of it.__

3. When it is Lee's turn to speak, she feels

   __X__ nervous.

   _____ happy.

   _____ cross.

4. Why did Sharla's face turn red when Mrs. Holt asked about how they completed their project?

   __She was embarrassed.__

5. What experiences have you had working with other people? Were there times when you didn't agree or get along? Write about it.

   __Answers will vary.__

47

Page 49

Vocabulary Skills

Write the words from the article that have these meanings.

1. not strong

   __weak__

2. being the only one of its kind

   __unique__

Listen to the sound of the **g** in *magma*. Circle the words below that have the same sound as the **g** in *magma*. (The sound may be at the beginning, middle, or end of the word.)

3. change   (flag)

4. (garden)   page

5. (began)   danger

6. gentle   (goose)

The words below are broken into syllables. Sound out each syllable. Then, write the word and say it to yourself as you write.

7. vol/ca/nol/o/gist __volcanologist__

8. e/rup/tions __eruptions__

Reading Skills

In nonfiction writing, the author sometimes calls attention to words that the reader may not know. Those words appear in **bold** type. The author usually gives the meaning of the bold word in the same sentence.

Below are the bold words from the article. Write the meaning of each word.

1. molten   __melted__

2. expand   __get bigger__

3. fissures   __cracks__

4. active   __experience eruptions__

5. dormant   __inactive__

Write **F** next to each sentence that is a fact. Write **O** next to each sentence that is an opinion.

6. __O__ Volcanic eruptions are one of the most striking natural events.

7. __O__ A volcanic eruption is more frightening than a hurricane.

8. __F__ Volcanoes are located in many places in the world.

Study Skills

1. What does the illustration show?

   __the inside of a volcano__

2. Trace with your finger the path that magma would take from under Earth's crust to the surface. Describe the path in your own words.

   __Answers will vary.__

49

Answer Key

Page 51

Vocabulary Skills

In each group below, circle the three words that belong together.

1. (math) (science) backpack (reading)
2. (weekend) weather (day) (month)
3. lunch (eyebrow) (knee) (hand)
4. (afternoon) (morning) (evening) activity

Circle the correct letters to complete each word. Write the letters in the blank.

5. The next unit is about the natural w__or__ld.
   er   (or)   ir
6. The classroom is always busy in the m__or__ning.
   ar   (or)   er
7. She made a c__ir__cle with her arms.
   or   er   (ir)
8. The weath__er__ chart is the first part of the day.
   (er)   ur   ir

Reading Skills

Write the best word to complete each sentence below.

1. The students were especially __noisy__ on Monday morning. (noisy, rosy, nosy)
2. Miss Eller wrote the topic on the __board__. (body, break, board)
3. The teacher waved her __arms__ all around. (aims, aches, arms)
4. Zach was only __kidding__ about the grasshopper's knees. (kind, kidding, kitten)
5. What do Miss Eller's students do as they begin their day? Find five details from the story and list them in order.
   __empty backpacks, sign__
   __in, morning math__
   __problems, Morning__
   __Meeting, weather chart__
6. What do you think will happen after lunch, when the students meet to talk about their new unit?
   __Answers will vary.__

51

Page 53

Vocabulary Skills

Write the words from the story that have these meanings.

1. feeling a need to drink liquid
   __thirsty__ Par. 1
2. plainly
   __simply__ Par. 2
3. a very short period of time
   __moment__ Par. 5

Match each word in the first list with its antonym in the second list. Write the letter in the blank.

4. __c__ narrow   a. same
5. __d__ wild   b. fuzzy
6. __a__ different c. wide
7. __b__ bald   d. tame

Have you heard this saying?

I before e, except after c, or when rhyming with hay, as in neighbor and weigh.

The words in this box follow the rule.

| believe | ceiling | sleigh |

Use the words to complete the sentences.

8. The snow made a __sleigh__ ride possible.
9. You wouldn't __believe__ me even if I told you.
10. I stared at the crack in the __ceiling__.

Reading Skills

1. Which of the students' ideas do you like best? Write why.
   __Answers will vary.__
2. Write **R** next to the sentences that tell about what Miss Eller's students could do for their study of the natural world. Write **M** next to the sentences that are about made-up things.
   __M__ Isaac goes to the South Pole.
   __R__ Tina collects seeds.
   __R__ Justin sets up a bird feeder.
   __M__ Megan climbs the Alps.
3. What does this sentence from the story tell you about Miss Eller?
   "Miss Eller's quiet presence at the meeting rug was a signal for everyone to settle down and join her."
   __Answers will vary.__
4. Look for another sentence that tells you something about Miss Eller. What does it tell you?
   __Answers will vary.__

53

Page 55

Vocabulary Skills

Write the words from the story that have these meanings.

1. to make less wide or broad
   __narrow__ Par. 2
2. hairy, furry
   __fuzzy__ Par. 4

Choose the word that correctly completes the sentence and write it in the blank.

3. Miss Eller hoped the __whole__ class would buy the idea. (hole, whole)
4. The students will not be __bored__ if they choose their own topics. (board, bored)
5. Miss Eller really wants the students to __sell__ their ideas. (cell, sell)

Reading Skills

1. This story is mostly about
   __X__ solving a problem.
   _____ how to do research.
   _____ getting ready for school.
2. Why does Miss Eller let the students offer so many ideas?
   __She wants them to help__
   __decide what they study.__

3. Write in your own words what Miss Eller's solution is.
   __Answers will vary.__

Study Skills

To find the meaning of a word, look in a dictionary. Some words have more than one meaning. Look at the words and their meanings below. Answer the questions.

solo a performance or action done by one person

solution 1 the answer to a problem; 2 a mixture of two or more substances

solve to find the solution to

1. Which word means "to find the solution to"?
   __solve__
2. What is a solo?
   __something done by one__
   __person__
3. Which meaning of *solution* is used in this sentence?
   Letting the students decide was a perfect solution.
   __the first meaning__

55

Page 57

Vocabulary Skills

Circle the word that correctly completes each sentence. Write the word in the blank.

1. A mouse may live in the forest, or it may live in your __house__.
   (house)   hose   how
2. Insect eaters might dig in the ground for their __food__.
   felt   fair   (food)
3. Rodents use their strong front teeth to __gnaw__ on hard nuts and branches.
   (gnaw)   blow   growl
4. The most famous rodents are probably __beavers__ because of the dams they make.
   trees   (beavers)   secrets

When a word has one consonant between two vowels, the break between the syllables depends on the first vowel. If the vowel has a long sound, as in *beaver*, the consonant goes with the second syllable: *bea / ver*. If the vowel has a short sound, as in *body*, the consonant stays with the first syllable: *bod / y*. For each word below, draw a line to divide the word into syllables.

5. e a / t e r s   6. m a n / y
7. f e / m a l e   8. s t e a d / y
9. l e a f / y

Reading Skills

1. What four common characteristics do mammals have?
   __warm blood__
   __backbones__
   __milk fed to babies__
   __hair or fur__

In the article, the author showed some words in bold type. The meanings of those words are given as well. Find the meanings of the words and write them here.

2. habitat __natural conditions__
3. insectivores __insect eaters__
4. rodents __gnawing animals__
5. carnivores __meat eaters__

57

Answer Key

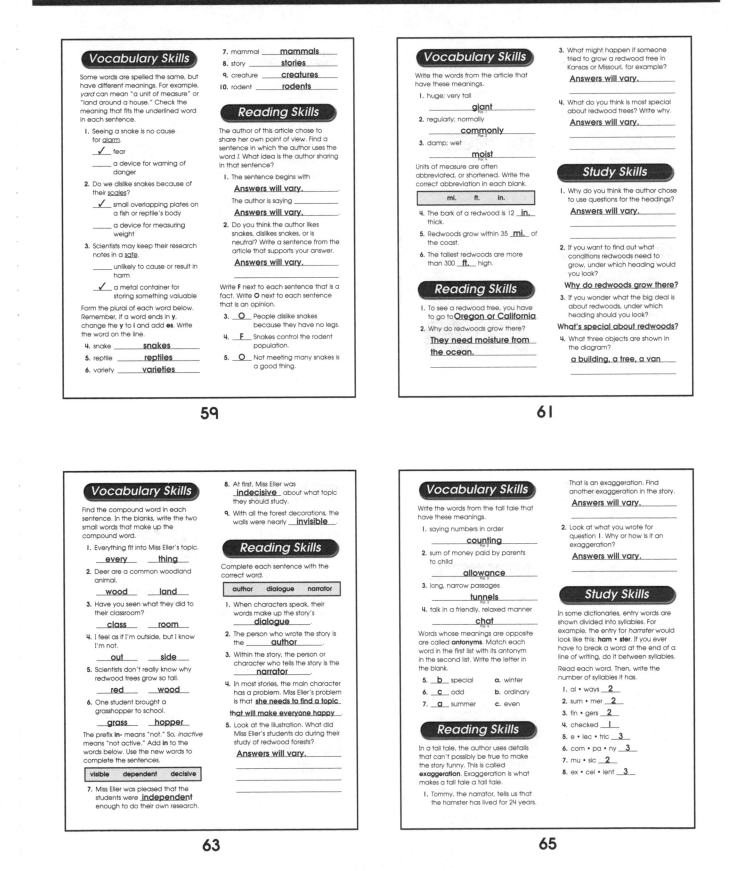

Vocabulary Skills

Some words are spelled the same, but have different meanings. For example, *yard* can mean "a unit of measure" or "land around a house." Check the meaning that fits the underlined word in each sentence.

1. Seeing a snake is no cause for <u>alarm</u>.
   - ✓ fear
   - _____ a device for warning of danger

2. Do we dislike snakes because of their <u>scales</u>?
   - ✓ small overlapping plates on a fish or reptile's body
   - _____ a device for measuring weight

3. Scientists may keep their research notes in a <u>safe</u>.
   - _____ unlikely to cause or result in harm
   - ✓ a metal container for storing something valuable

Form the plural of each word below. Remember, if a word ends in **y**, change the **y** to **i** and add **es**. Write the word on the line.

4. snake _____ **snakes**
5. reptile _____ **reptiles**
6. variety _____ **varieties**
7. mammal _____ **mammals**
8. story _____ **stories**
9. creature _____ **creatures**
10. rodent _____ **rodents**

Reading Skills

The author of this article chose to share her own point of view. Find a sentence in which the author uses the word *I*. What idea is the author sharing in that sentence?

1. The sentence begins with
   Answers will vary.
   The author is saying _____
   Answers will vary.

2. Do you think the author likes snakes, dislikes snakes, or is neutral? Write a sentence from the article that supports your answer.
   Answers will vary.

Write **F** next to each sentence that is a fact. Write **O** next to each sentence that is an opinion.

3. **O** People dislike snakes because they have no legs.
4. **F** Snakes control the rodent population.
5. **O** Not meeting many snakes is a good thing.

59

Vocabulary Skills

Write the words from the article that have these meanings.

1. huge; very tall
   giant Par. 1
2. regularly; normally
   commonly Par. 2
3. damp; wet
   moist Par. 4

Units of measure are often abbreviated, or shortened. Write the correct abbreviation in each blank.

| mi. | ft. | in. |

4. The bark of a redwood is 12 **in.** thick.
5. Redwoods grow within 35 **mi.** of the coast.
6. The tallest redwoods are more than 300 **ft.** high.

Reading Skills

1. To see a redwood tree, you have to go to **Oregon or California**.
2. Why do redwoods grow there?
   They need moisture from the ocean.

3. What might happen if someone tried to grow a redwood tree in Kansas or Missouri, for example?
   Answers will vary.

4. What do you think is most special about redwood trees? Write why.
   Answers will vary.

Study Skills

1. Why do you think the author chose to use questions for the headings?
   Answers will vary.

2. If you want to find out what conditions redwoods need to grow, under which heading would you look?
   Why do redwoods grow there?

3. If you wonder what the big deal is about redwoods, under which heading should you look?
   What's special about redwoods?

4. What three objects are shown in the diagram?
   a building, a tree, a van

61

Vocabulary Skills

Find the compound word in each sentence. In the blanks, write the two small words that make up the compound word.

1. Everything fit into Miss Eller's topic.
   every **thing**
2. Deer are a common woodland animal.
   wood **land**
3. Have you seen what they did to their classroom?
   class **room**
4. I feel as if I'm outside, but I know I'm not.
   out **side**
5. Scientists don't really know why redwood trees grow so tall.
   red **wood**
6. One student brought a grasshopper to school.
   grass **hopper**

The prefix **in-** means "not." So, *inactive* means "not active." Add **in** to the words below. Use the new words to complete the sentences.

| visible | dependent | decisive |

7. Miss Eller was pleased that the students were **independent** enough to do their own research.

8. At first, Miss Eller was **indecisive** about what topic they should study.
9. With all the forest decorations, the walls were nearly **invisible**.

Reading Skills

Complete each sentence with the correct word.

| author | dialogue | narrator |

1. When characters speak, their words make up the story's
   dialogue .
2. The person who wrote the story is the **author** .
3. Within the story, the person or character who tells the story is the **narrator** .
4. In most stories, the main character has a problem. Miss Eller's problem is that **she needs to find a topic that will make everyone happy** .
5. Look at the illustration. What did Miss Eller's students do during their study of redwood forests?
   Answers will vary.

63

Vocabulary Skills

Write the words from the tall tale that have these meanings.

1. saying numbers in order
   counting Par. 1
2. sum of money paid by parents to child
   allowance Par. 3
3. long, narrow passages
   tunnels Par. 3
4. talk in a friendly, relaxed manner
   chat Par. 4

Words whose meanings are opposite are called **antonyms**. Match each word in the first list with its antonym in the second list. Write the letter in the blank.

5. **b** special   a. winter
6. **c** odd   b. ordinary
7. **a** summer   c. even

Reading Skills

In a tall tale, the author uses details that can't possibly be true to make the story funny. This is called **exaggeration**. Exaggeration is what makes a tall tale a tall tale.

1. Tommy, the narrator, tells us that the hamster has lived for 24 years.

That is an exaggeration. Find another exaggeration in the story.
Answers will vary.

2. Look at what you wrote for question 1. How or why is it an exaggeration?
Answers will vary.

Study Skills

In some dictionaries, entry words are shown divided into syllables. For example, the entry for *hamster* would look like this: **ham • ster**. If you ever have to break a word at the end of a line of writing, do it between syllables.

Read each word. Then, write the number of syllables it has.

1. al • ways **2**
2. sum • mer **2**
3. fin • gers **2**
4. checked **1**
5. e • lec • tric **3**
6. com • pa • ny **3**
7. mu • sic **2**
8. ex • cel • lent **3**

65

Answer Key

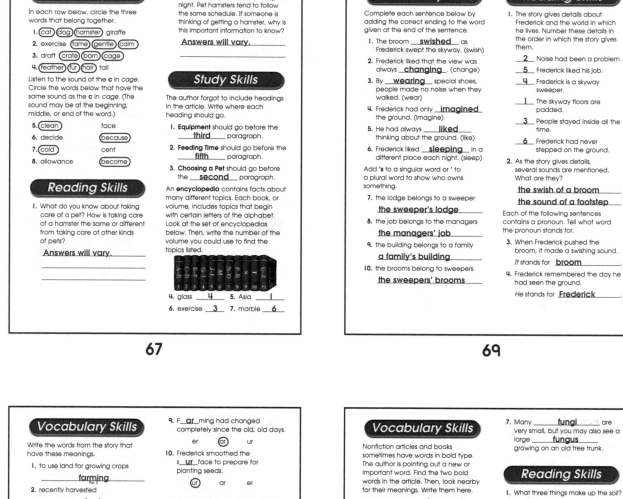

Page 67

Vocabulary Skills

In each row below, circle the three words that belong together.

1. (cat) (dog) (hamster) giraffe
2. exercise (tame) (gentle) (calm)
3. draft (crate) (barn) (cage)
4. (feather) (fur) (hair) tail

Listen to the sound of the **c** in *cage*. Circle the words below that have the same sound as the **c** in *cage*. (The sound may be at the beginning, middle, or end of the word.)

5. (clean)   face
6. decide   (because)
7. (cold)   cent
8. allowance   (become)

Reading Skills

1. What do you know about taking care of a pet? How is taking care of a hamster the same or different from taking care of other kinds of pets?

   Answers will vary.

2. In the wild, hamsters sleep during the day and gather food during the night. Pet hamsters tend to follow the same schedule. If someone is thinking of getting a hamster, why is this important information to know?

   Answers will vary.

Study Skills

The author forgot to include headings in the article. Write where each heading should go.

1. **Equipment** should go before the **third** paragraph.
2. **Feeding Time** should go before the **fifth** paragraph.
3. **Choosing a Pet** should go before the **second** paragraph.

An **encyclopedia** contains facts about many different topics. Each book, or volume, includes topics that begin with certain letters of the alphabet. Look at the set of encyclopedias below. Then, write the number of the volume you could use to find the topics listed.

4. glass **4**   5. Asia **1**
6. exercise **3**   7. marble **6**

Page 69

Vocabulary Skills

Complete each sentence below by adding the correct ending to the word given at the end of the sentence.

1. The broom **swished** as Frederick swept the skyway. (swish)
2. Frederick liked that the view was always **changing**. (change)
3. By **wearing** special shoes, people made no noise when they walked. (wear)
4. Frederick had only **imagined** the ground. (imagine)
5. He had always **liked** thinking about the ground. (like)
6. Frederick liked **sleeping** in a different place each night. (sleep)

Add **'s** to a singular word or **'** to a plural word to show who owns something.

7. the lodge belongs to a sweeper
   the sweeper's lodge
8. the job belongs to the managers
   the managers' job
9. the building belongs to a family
   a family's building
10. the brooms belong to sweepers
    the sweepers' brooms

Reading Skills

1. The story gives details about Frederick and the world in which he lives. Number these details in the order in which the story gives them.

   2 Noise had been a problem.
   5 Frederick liked his job.
   4 Frederick is a skyway sweeper.
   1 The skyway floors are padded.
   3 People stayed inside all the time.
   6 Frederick had never stepped on the ground.

2. As the story gives details, several sounds are mentioned. What are they?

   the swish of a broom
   the sound of a footstep

Each of the following sentences contains a pronoun. Tell what word the pronoun stands for.

3. When Frederick pushed the broom, it made a swishing sound.
   It stands for **broom**
4. Frederick remembered the day he had seen the ground.
   He stands for **Frederick**

Page 71

Vocabulary Skills

Write the words from the story that have these meanings.

1. to use land for growing crops
   farming Par. 1
2. recently harvested
   fresh Par. 1
3. to give or make available
   supply Par. 2
4. stated; gave an opinion
   commented Par. 3

Circle the word that is a synonym of the underlined word in each sentence.

5. Frederick wondered what <u>sound</u> real dirt made.
   clank   (noise)   rattle
6. Making people happy with his crops <u>pleased</u> Frederick.
   entertained   worried   (delighted)
7. Frederick could never get used to that <u>faint</u> chemical odor.
   thin   pale   (weak)

Circle the correct letters to complete each word. Write the letters in the blank.

8. All that Frederick could think about was d**ir**t.
   ur   er   (ir)

9. F**ar**ming had changed completely since the old, old days.
   er   (ar)   ur
10. Frederick smoothed the s**ur**face to prepare for planting seeds.
    (ur)   ar   er

Reading Skills

1. Write **R** next to the sentences that tell about something real. Write **M** next to the sentences that are about made-up things.

   M People do not know what dirt feels like.
   M The whole world is covered up with buildings.
   R People grow vegetables in gardens.
   M People stay indoors and never have to go outside.

In some stories, the problem is obvious. Maybe the character breaks an arm and has to learn how to write with the other hand, or something like that. In this story, the problem is not as obvious.

2. What problem does this character have?

   He has never felt real dirt
   and wonders what it's like.

Page 73

Vocabulary Skills

Nonfiction articles and books sometimes have words in bold type. The author is pointing out a new or important word. Find the two bold words in the article. Then, look nearby for their meanings. Write them here.

1. Bold word: **fragments**
   Meaning: **tiny pieces**
2. Bold word: **humus**
   Meaning: **a dark, slightly sticky substance that helps plants grow**

Sound out each syllable. Then, write the word and say it to yourself as you write.

3. min/er/als **minerals**
4. par/ti/cles **particles**
5. or/gan/isms **organisms**

To make the plural of most English words, add **s** or **es**. Here are two words that don't follow the pattern. Read each sentence. Then, write the correct word in each blank.

| bacterium—bacteria |
| fungus—fungi |

6. There are so many millions of **bacteria** that we seldom talk about just one **bacterium**.

7. Many **fungi** are very small, but you may also see a large **fungus** growing on an old tree trunk.

Reading Skills

1. What three things make up the soil?
   minerals
   remains of dead plants and animals
   living organisms
2. When was the last time you dug in the soil? What did you see there?
   Answers will vary.
3. Now, look at the picture on this page. What do you see there?
   Answers will vary.
4. How does this compare with what you saw when you dug in the soil yourself?
   Answers will vary.

Answer Key

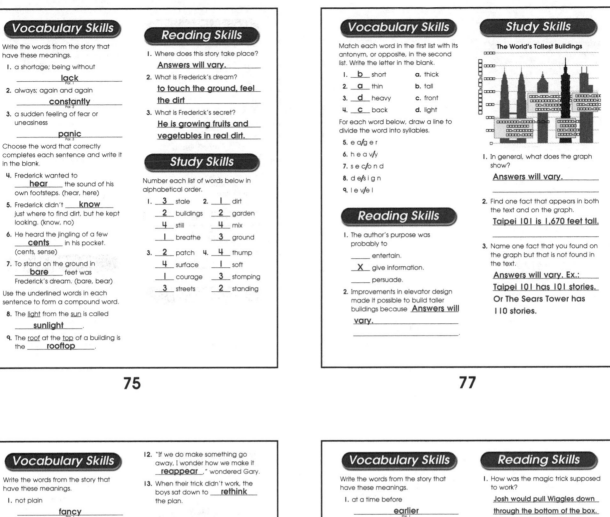

Page 75

Vocabulary Skills

Write the words from the story that have these meanings.

1. a shortage; being without
   lack _{Par. I}

2. always; again and again
   constantly _{Par. 2}

3. a sudden feeling of fear or uneasiness
   panic _{Par. 3}

Choose the word that correctly completes each sentence and write it in the blank.

4. Frederick wanted to **hear** the sound of his own footsteps. (hear, here)

5. Frederick didn't **know** just where to find dirt, but he kept looking. (know, no)

6. He heard the jingling of a few **cents** in his pocket. (cents, sense)

7. To stand on the ground in **bare** feet was Frederick's dream. (bare, bear)

Use the underlined words in each sentence to form a compound word.

8. The light from the sun is called **sunlight**.

9. The roof at the top of a building is the **rooftop**.

Reading Skills

1. Where does this story take place?
   Answers will vary.

2. What is Frederick's dream?
   to touch the ground, feel the dirt

3. What is Frederick's secret?
   He is growing fruits and vegetables in real dirt.

Study Skills

Number each list of words below in alphabetical order.

1. **3** stale   2. **1** dirt
   2 buildings   **2** garden
   4 still   **4** mix
   1 breathe   **3** ground

3. **2** patch   4. **4** thump
   4 surface   **1** soft
   1 courage   **3** stomping
   3 streets   **2** standing

75

Page 77

Vocabulary Skills

Match each word in the first list with its antonym, or opposite, in the second list. Write the letter in the blank.

1. **b** short   a. thick
2. **a** thin   b. tall
3. **d** heavy   c. front
4. **c** back   d. light

For each word below, draw a line to divide the word into syllables.

5. e a/g e r
6. h e a v/y
7. s e c/o n d
8. d e/s i g n
9. l e v/e l

Reading Skills

1. The author's purpose was probably to
   _____ entertain.
   X give information.
   _____ persuade.

2. Improvements in elevator design made it possible to build taller buildings because **Answers will vary.**

Study Skills

The World's Tallest Buildings

1. In general, what does the graph show?
   Answers will vary.

2. Find one fact that appears in both the text and on the graph.
   Taipei 101 is 1,670 feet tall.

3. Name one fact that you found on the graph but that is not found in the text.
   Answers will vary. Ex.: Taipei 101 has 101 stories. Or The Sears Tower has 110 stories.

77

Page 79

Vocabulary Skills

Write the words from the story that have these meanings.

1. not plain
   fancy _{Par. I}

2. flowing from a container
   spilling _{Par. 4}

3. droop
   wilt _{Par. 6}

4. jammed; caught in a position
   stuck _{Par. 8}

Form the plural of each word below by adding **s** or **es**. Write the word on the line.

5. arm   **arms**
6. table   **tables**
7. branch   **branches**
8. vase   **vases**
9. box   **boxes**
10. flower   **flowers**

The prefix **re-** means "again." So, *redo* means "do again." Use the words below to complete each sentence. Write the words in the blanks.

| reappear | reinvent | rethink |

11. The boys wished they could **reinvent** what the great magicians had done.

12. "If we do make something go away, I wonder how we make it **reappear**," wondered Gary.

13. When their trick didn't work, the boys sat down to **rethink** the plan.

Reading Skills

1. This story is mostly about
   X two boys trying to do a magic trick.
   _____ a boy teaching another boy a magic trick.
   _____ how to do a magic trick.

2. Josh got wet because **the flower vase tipped and spilled**

3. Why was Josh under the table?
   to pull the flower vase down; to make the flowers disappear

4. What do you think will happen next?
   Answers will vary.

79

Page 81

Vocabulary Skills

Write the words from the story that have these meanings.

1. at a time before
   earlier _{Par. I}

2. moved on hands and knees
   crawled _{Par. 4}

3. shared the same view
   agreed _{Par. 11}

A **contraction** is one word that stands for two words. Write a contraction for each pair of words below.

4. could not   **couldn't**
5. she will   **she'll**
6. what is   **what's**
7. he would   **he'd**

8. Now write a sentence using the contraction you wrote for question 4, above.
   Answers will vary. Ex.: He couldn't believe they had done it.

In each row below, circle the three words that belong together.

9. snake (rabbit)(hamster)(mouse)
10. (cape)(hat)(wand) briefcase
11. (garden)(tree) table (grass)

Reading Skills

1. How was the magic trick supposed to work?
   Josh would pull Wiggles down through the bottom of the box.

2. What actually happened?
   Wiggles actually got out without the boys noticing.

Write the best word to complete each sentence below.

3. They should have thought of Wiggles **sooner**. (brighter, sooner, calmer)

4. The magic words made the boys **laugh** so hard. (laugh, lame, learn)

5. It made Gary feel like a real magician when he **waved** his cape. (waved, cried, tapped)

6. The boys couldn't **believe** Wiggles was gone. (agree, scramble, believe)

7. Write **R** next to the sentences that tell about something real. Write **M** next to the sentences that are about made-up things.
   R Rabbits eat lettuce.
   M Rabbits disappear and reappear.
   R Magicians say magic words.

81

Answer Key

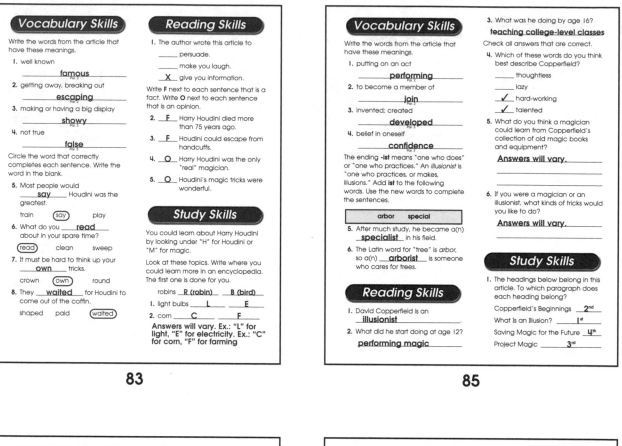

Page 83

Vocabulary Skills

Write the words from the article that have these meanings.

1. well known
   famous *Par. 2*
2. getting away, breaking out
   escaping *Par. 2*
3. making or having a big display
   showy *Par. 3*
4. not true
   false *Par. 5*

Circle the word that correctly completes each sentence. Write the word in the blank.

5. Most people would **say** Houdini was the greatest.
   train (say) play
6. What do you **read** about in your spare time?
   (read) clean sweep
7. It must be hard to think up your **own** tricks.
   crown (own) round
8. They **waited** for Houdini to come out of the coffin.
   shaped paid (waited)

Reading Skills

1. The author wrote this article to
   _____ persuade.
   _____ make you laugh.
   X give you information.

Write F next to each sentence that is a fact. Write O next to each sentence that is an opinion.

2. **F** Harry Houdini died more than 75 years ago.
3. **F** Houdini could escape from handcuffs.
4. **O** Harry Houdini was the only "real" magician.
5. **O** Houdini's magic tricks were wonderful.

Study Skills

You could learn about Harry Houdini by looking under "H" for Houdini or "M" for magic. Write where you could learn more in an encyclopedia. The first one is done for you.

robins **R (robin)**   **B (bird)**
1. light bulbs   **L**   **E**
2. corn   **C**   **F**

Answers will vary. Ex.: "L" for light, "E" for electricity. Ex.: "C" for corn, "F" for farming

Page 85

Vocabulary Skills

Write the words from the article that have these meanings.

1. putting on an act
   performing *Par. 2*
2. to become a member of
   join *Par. 2*
3. invented; created
   developed *Par. 2*
4. belief in oneself
   confidence *Par. 3*

The ending -**ist** means "one who does" or "one who practices." An *illusionist* is "one who practices, or makes, illusions." Add **ist** to the following words. Use the new words to complete the sentences.

| arbor | special |

5. After much study, he became a(n) **specialist** in his field.
6. The Latin word for "tree" is *arbor*, so a(n) **arborist** is someone who cares for trees.

Reading Skills

1. David Copperfield is an **illusionist**.
2. What did he start doing at age 12?
   performing magic
3. What was he doing by age 16?
   teaching college-level classes

Check all answers that are correct.

4. Which of these words do you think best describe Copperfield?
   _____ thoughtless
   _____ lazy
   ✓ hard-working
   ✓ talented

5. What do you think a magician could learn from Copperfield's collection of old magic books and equipment?
   Answers will vary.

6. If you were a magician or an illusionist, what kinds of tricks would you like to do?
   Answers will vary.

Study Skills

1. The headings below belong in this article. To which paragraph does each heading belong?
   Copperfield's Beginnings **2nd**
   What Is an Illusion? **1st**
   Saving Magic for the Future **4th**
   Project Magic **3rd**

Page 87

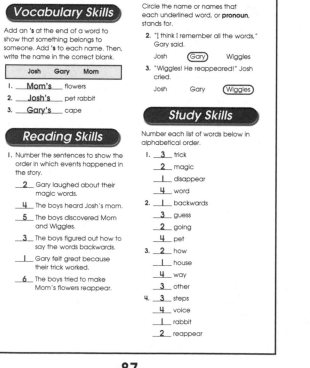

Vocabulary Skills

Add an '**s** at the end of a word to show that something belongs to someone. Add '**s** to each name. Then, write the name in the correct blank.

| Josh | Gary | Mom |

1. **Mom's** flowers
2. **Josh's** pet rabbit
3. **Gary's** cape

Reading Skills

1. Number the sentences to show the order in which events happened in the story.
   2 Gary laughed about their magic words.
   4 The boys heard Josh's mom.
   5 The boys discovered Mom and Wiggles.
   3 The boys figured out how to say the words backwards.
   1 Gary felt great because their trick worked.
   6 The boys tried to make Mom's flowers reappear.

Circle the name or names that each underlined word, or **pronoun**, stands for.

2. "I think I remember all the words," Gary said.
   Josh (Gary) Wiggles
3. "Wiggles! He reappeared!" Josh cried.
   Josh Gary (Wiggles)

Study Skills

Number each list of words below in alphabetical order.

1. **3** trick
   2 magic
   1 disappear
   4 word
2. **1** backwards
   3 guess
   2 going
   4 pet
3. **2** how
   1 house
   4 way
   3 other
4. **3** steps
   4 voice
   1 rabbit
   2 reappear

Page 89

Vocabulary Skills

Write the words from the story that have these meanings.

1. rough, bouncy
   bumpy *Par. 2*
2. store that sells food
   grocery *Par. 6*
3. gathered a crop
   harvested *Par. 7*
4. according to the rules
   fair *Par. 4*

Make a check next to the meaning that fits the underlined word in each sentence.

5. Be careful not to <u>trip</u> on the rock.
   ✓ to stumble
   _____ a journey
6. One building was a <u>store</u>.
   _____ to collect and save items
   ✓ a place to buy things
7. Each house had its own <u>well</u>.
   ✓ a hole dug for water
   _____ an exclamation
8. The children did not have a <u>fair</u> day for their field trip.
   _____ light-colored, as hair or skin
   ✓ sunny and clear, without wind

Reading Skills

1. The children notice that the town of Rockville is **quite small**.
2. What three sights do the children see out the bus window? Write the parts of the sentences from the story that tell you.
   "This is a little town...
   ...tall, dry cornfields...
   ...a long gray wall

The place where a story happens is the **setting**. An author might describe how a place looks, how it feels, or how it smells. The author of this story described the setting of this story in the first paragraph. Answer these questions.

3. During what time of year does this story take place?
   October
4. What kind of day is it?
   windy
5. What detail tells you that it might be a little chilly?
   It is windy, and the children have jackets on.

Answer Key

Vocabulary Skills

Match each word in the first list with its antonym in the second list. Write the letter in the blank.

1. __a__ behind   a. ahead
2. __c__ noise   b. loud
3. __d__ long   c. silence
4. __b__ quiet   d. short

Form a contraction from each pair of words below. Write the contraction.

5. it is ___it's___
6. there is ___there's___
7. did not ___didn't___
8. would not ___wouldn't___
9. you are ___you're___
10. do not ___don't___

Reading Skills

Write **T** if the sentence is true. Write **F** if the sentence is false.

1. __F__ The children saw a castle.
2. __F__ The wall was on only one side of the bus.
3. __T__ Jason had a book on the bus.
4. __F__ The walls surrounded a lake.

5. What does this story tell you about Jason? You may check more than one.

   ✓ He likes to joke around.
   ✓ He is interested in history.
   ___ He doesn't get along with Steven.
   ___ He has never been on a field trip before.

Study Skills

In a dictionary, you will find two words at the top of each page. These are **guide words**. The first guide word shows what the first entry on the page is. The last guide word is the last entry word on the page. All the other words on the page fall in alphabetical order between the two guide words.

Look at the guide words below. Then, check the words that would fall on that dictionary page.

wall / whisper

1. ✓ wet
2. ✓ wax
3. ___ wick
4. ✓ west
5. ___ worth
6. ___ wrist
7. ✓ waffle
8. ___ wilt

91

Vocabulary Skills

Circle the word that is a synonym of the underlined word in each sentence.

1. It was a huge job to <u>connect</u> the old parts of the wall.
   (join) build move
2. Building the wall must have been hard <u>work</u>.
   faith strength (labor)
3. Even with the wall, China was <u>invaded</u> a number of times.
   improved built (attacked)
4. What else can you think of that is a great human <u>feat</u>?
   building (accomplishment) wall

Write the correct abbreviation in each blank.

mi.	ft.

5. If you are standing on the Great Wall, you could be about 25 ___ft.___ above the ground.
6. The top of the wall was made 12 ___ft.___ wide so soldiers and carts could travel along the wall.
7. If every curve of the wall is measured, it is 1,500 ___mi.___ long.
8. If a straight line were drawn from one end of the wall to the other, the line would be 1,200 ___mi.___ long.

Reading Skills

1. The Great Wall of China was built
   ___ as a place for soldiers to live.
   __X__ to protect China.
   ___ to honor the emperors.

Write the best word to complete each sentence below.

2. It took hundreds of years to ___build___ the Great Wall of China. (move, build, climb)
3. Peasants were poor ___people___ who did not have farms. (people, emperors, walls)
4. Today, people may ___visit___ the Great Wall and walk along it. (twist, visit, hear)

Study Skills

1. What does the map show?
   ___China, the city of Beijing,___
   ___and the Great Wall___
2. Based on the map, describe how the Great Wall might look from high above earth.
   ___Answers will vary.___

93

Vocabulary Skills

Write the words from the article that have these meanings.

1. divide, keep apart
   ___separate___
2. small or gentle hill
   ___slope___
3. had different opinions
   ___disagreed___

Circle the correct letters to complete each word. Write the letters in the blank.

4. The people whose names are on the wall all s___er___ved during the Vietnam War.
   ir (er) ur
5. The names are c___ar___ved into the black stone.
   or (ar) er

Reading Skills

1. This article is mostly about
   ___ Maya Ying Lin.
   ___ the Vietnam War.
   __X__ the Vietnam Veterans Memorial.
2. The Wall was completed in ___1982___

3. How many names are on the wall?
   ___58, 245___
4. Why was the Vietnam Veterans Memorial built?
   ___to remember everyone who___
   ___served in the Vietnam War___
5. Look at the picture of the wall. Then, look back at the design requirements. Write how you think the Wall meets one of those requirements.
   ___Answers will vary.___
   _____
   _____

Study Skills

In what volume of the encyclopedia would you look to find these topics? Write the volume number.

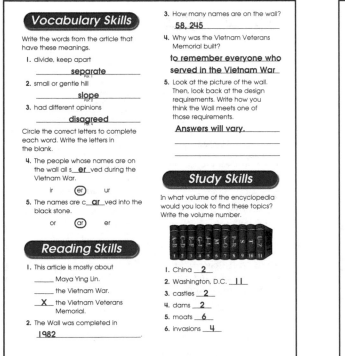

1. China ___2___
2. Washington, D.C. ___11___
3. castles ___2___
4. dams ___2___
5. moats ___6___
6. invasions ___4___

95

Vocabulary Skills

Use the words below to complete the sentences. Use each word twice.

wind	spoke

1. Don't forget to ___wind___ the clock.
2. When Mrs. Hoff ___spoke___, everyone listened.
3. My bicycle wheel has a broken ___spoke___.
4. I like to hear the ___wind___ in the trees.

To show that something happened in the past, most words add **ed** to the end. Some words, however, don't follow that pattern. For example, the past form of *sing* is *sang*. Use the words below to complete the sentences.

| catch—caught |
| teach—taught |
| freeze—froze |

5. Mrs. Hoff will ___teach___ us about the farm, just as she was ___taught___ to do.
6. Did it ___freeze___ last night? I nearly ___froze___ while I waited for the bus this morning.
7. I would like to ___catch___ the wind, but I think it ___caught___ me first.

Reading Skills

1. What kind of day is it?
   ___a windy day___
2. What are the children going to learn about?
   ___how people farmed and___
   ___lived in the 1860s___
3. How is Jesse's clothing different from Mrs. Hoff's?
   ___Mrs. Hoff is in a long dress, apron,___
   ___and a little cap. Jesse has on___
   ___jeans, a shirt, jacket, and sneakers.___
4. Have you ever been on a field trip? What kinds of things did you do?
   ___Answers will vary.___
   _____
   _____
   _____
5. What do you think will happen next?
   ___Answers will vary.___
   _____
   _____
   _____

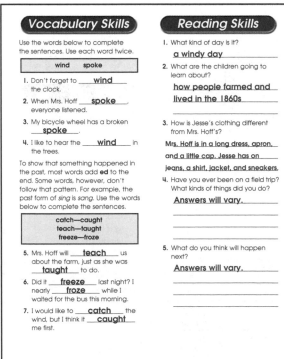

97

Answer Key

Page 99

Vocabulary Skills

When a short word has an **ing** ending, the syllable break comes between the word and its ending. If the final consonant is doubled, as in *stepping*, the syllables break between the double consonant: *step/ping*. For each word below, draw a line to divide the word into syllables.

1. f l a p/p i n g
2. h o n k/i n g
3. s t a n d/i n g
4. t i p/p i n g
5. g r o w/i n g

Reading Skills

1. In the barn, the students saw <u>a man and some sheep</u>.

In this story, the author uses **dialogue** to move the story along. For each piece of dialogue below, fill in the name of the character who said it. Then, write what the dialogue tells you about the character or the story.

2. "I was just checking to see how the wool was growing."

<u>Mr. Brown; He knows</u>
<u>about wool and sheep.</u>

3. "Does wool really grow?"

<u>a student; The student</u>
<u>doesn't know about wool</u>
<u>or sheep.</u>

4. "I clipped these sheep just about down to the skin in spring."

<u>Mr. Brown; Mr. Brown is the</u>
<u>one who clipped the</u>
<u>sheep's wool.</u>

5. Write **R** next to the sentences that tell about something real. Write **M** next to the sentences that are about made-up things.

   __R__ Farmers raise sheep.

   __R__ A sheep's coat is wool.

   __M__ Sheep come in many bright colors, just like yarn.

6. Number the sentences to show the order in which wool is processed.

   __3__ Card the wool.

   __6__ Weave the wool.

   __1__ Clip the wool.

   __5__ Spin the wool.

   __2__ Wash the wool.

   __4__ Dye the wool.

99

Page 101

Vocabulary Skills

In each row below, circle the three words that belong together.

1. (stove) (sink) (oven) bed
2. cow (house) (barn) (shed)
3. (bread) apple (roll) (muffin)

Write the words from the story that have these meanings.

4. making a short, high-pitched sound

   ____squeaky____

5. the part of clothing that covers the arms

   ____sleeves____

6. cooked in an oven

   ____baked____

7. to cut something into thin pieces

   ____slice____

Use the underlined words in each sentence to form a compound word. Write the word on the line.

8. The <u>pile</u> of <u>wood</u> is on the porch.

   ____woodpile____

9. The <u>house</u> is at the center of the <u>farm</u>.

   ____farmhouse____

10. After plowing all day, the farmer had an <u>ache</u> in his <u>back</u>.

   ____backache____

Reading Skills

1. It's hot in the kitchen because the <u>wood stove is heating up the room</u>.

2. What does the woman mean when she says, "the stove is hungry"?

<u>She means that the fire is going out and</u>
<u>she needs more wood to keep it going.</u>

3. Is Steven eager to taste the bread? How can you tell?

<u>Yes; at first he likes the smell. At</u>
<u>the end he thinks, "with pleasure."</u>

Write **F** next to each sentence that is a fact. Write **O** next to each sentence that is an opinion.

4. __F__ Some people still bake their own bread.

5. __O__ Bread is best when baked in a wood stove.

6. __O__ All bread smells good when it's baking.

Circle the name or names that each underlined word, or **pronoun**, stands for.

7. Steven couldn't believe the smell coming from the kitchen as <u>he</u> walked across the back porch.

   (Steven)   smell   kitchen

8. Mrs. Mason held the squeaky screen door open. Steven and the rest of the group went through <u>it</u>.

   Mrs. Mason   (door)   group

101

Page 103

Vocabulary Skills

Make a check next to the meaning that fits the underlined word in each sentence.

1. The recipe says to <u>cream</u> the butter and sugar.

   __✓__ to beat or stir together

   _____ thick, fatty part of milk

2. I hope I <u>bowl</u> well today.

   _____ an open, usually round container

   __✓__ a game played by rolling a ball down an alley

3. It is <u>kind</u> of Mrs. Seeley to share her bread.

   __✓__ courteous or caring

   _____ a group or type of something

4. Her quilt is filled with <u>down</u>.

   _____ movement toward a lower level

   __✓__ soft, fluffy feathers

Recipes often use short forms, or **abbreviations**, of words. Look at the common recipe words in the box. Write each word next to the correct item from the recipe.

cups	package
Fahrenheit	tablespoons
minutes	teaspoons

5. 40–45 min.   ____minutes____

6. 6 T. butter   ____tablespoons____

7. 350° F   ____Fahrenheit____

8. 3 c. flour   ____cups____

9. 1 pkg. dry yeast   ____package____

10. 1½ tsp. salt   ____teaspoons____

Reading Skills

1. What did Evelyn Seeley do before she retired?

   <u>She owned a bakery.</u>

2. What does she do now that she's retired?

   <u>She bakes bread.</u>

3. Number the sentences to show the order of the steps in the bread recipe.

   __3__ Add eggs.

   __6__ Let rise.

   __4__ Add milk, flour, and salt.

   __1__ Put yeast in water.

   __5__ Add yeast.

   __2__ Cream butter and sugar.

103

Page 105

Vocabulary Skills

Write the words from the story that have these meanings.

1. where the arms join the body

   ____shoulder____

2. moved across or sideways

   ____slid____

3. covered with a mass of hair or fur

   ____fuzzy____

4. put one's arms around

   ____hugged____

Match each word in the first list with its antonym in the second list. Write the letter in the blank.

5. __d__ tall   a. sour
6. __b__ huge   b. tiny
7. __c__ different   c. same
8. __a__ sweet   d. short

Write the past form of each action word below.

9. wave   ____waved____
10. laugh   ____laughed____
11. love   ____loved____
12. enjoy   ____enjoyed____
13. curl   ____curled____

Reading Skills

1. This story is mostly about

   _____ what the students learned on their field trip.

   __X__ what the students liked best about the field trip.

   _____ how much Jason liked the geese.

2. What is Jesse's favorite part about the farm?

   <u>the sheep</u>

3. Which student seems unsure about his favorite part?

   <u>Steven</u>

4. How can you tell?

   <u>First, he says the geese are his</u>
   <u>favorite, then the sheep, then</u>
   <u>he says the bread was perfect.</u>

5. Would you say that Steven is hard to please or easy to please? Explain.

   <u>Answers will vary.</u>

6. Where are the characters when they have this conversation?

   _____ in the barn

   _____ in the kitchen

   __X__ on the bus

   _____ outside

105

Answer Key

Page 107

Vocabulary Skills

These pairs of words sound the same, but have different meanings and spellings. Write the correct word from each pair to complete each sentence.

heard—herd	sea—see
know—no	sew—so

1. They could see __no__ reason for the traffic jam.
2. Jason wondered why __so__ many cars were here.
3. Jesse remembered the __herd__ of sheep at the farm.
4. She wished she could __see__ them again.

The prefix **dis-** means "not." It causes a word to mean the opposite of its base word. For example, *disagree* means "not agree."

Add **dis** to the words below. Use the new words to complete the sentences.

appear	comfort	honest

5. To tell a lie is __dishonest__.
6. The bus driver wished the traffic would __disappear__.
7. Sitting in traffic was annoying, but there was no real __discomfort__.

Sound out each syllable. Then, write the word and say it to yourself as you write.

8. dis/ap/pear/ing __disappearing__
9. an/noy/ing __annoying__
10. af/ter/noon __afternoon__

Reading Skills

Write the best word to complete each sentence below.

1. Up ahead, the line of cars went around a __curve__. (curve, ledge, movement)
2. Jason was worried about the bus being __late__. (hard, late, extra)
3. Steven wanted to __count__ the cars. (spin, read, count)
4. Have you ever been stuck in traffic? Write about how it felt.
   __Answers will vary.__
5. What might cause a traffic jam? List as many reasons as you can.
   __Answers will vary.__

107

Page 109

Vocabulary Skills

Write the words from the article that have these meanings.

1. paying out money
   __spending__ Par. 1
2. unplanned events
   __accidents__ Par. 2
3. all of the people in an area
   __population__ Par. 2

Form the plural of each word.

4. number __numbers__
5. inch __inches__
6. student __students__
7. change __changes__
8. graph __graphs__

Reading Skills

1. What kinds of things do we count? List two examples from the article.
   __Ex.: inches of rain, students,__
   __government spending, voters,__
   __traffic accidents, etc.__
2. What do we learn from counting things?
   __Ex.: to see how things need to__
   __change or how things are changing__

3. How do you think the information shown in this graph affects you and your community?
   __Answers will vary.__

Study Skills

Use the bar graph to answer these questions.

1. For each year, which is greater, the population or the number of cars?
   __the population__
2. If you want population data for 1950, would this graph help you? How can you tell?
   __No, the title says that the graph__
   __includes data only for 1960–2000.__
3. What was the population of the United States in 1970?
   __about 203.2 million, or just over 200 million__
4. How many cars were there in 1990?
   __about 133.7 million, or about 130 million__
5. Which two bars on the graph are almost the same height?
   __The number of cars for__
   __1990 and 2000 are almost__
   __the same.__

109

Page 111

Vocabulary Skills

Circle the word that is a synonym of the underlined word in each sentence.

1. The plants like soil that is moist.
   shaken   dripping   (damp)
2. The breeze is so weak it doesn't do any good.
   (faint)   healthy   medium
3. The shade moved close.
   (near)   wide   quickly

Add **'s** at the end of a word to show that something belongs to someone. Add **'s** to each name. Then, write the name in the correct blank.

Tatsu   Fujio

4. __Fujio's__ chalk
5. __Tatsu's__ sun picture

Say *count*. Notice the sound that the letters **ou** make. Circle the word that has the same sound as **ou** in *count*.

6. show   (cloudy)   blow   close
7. drawing   should   (outside)   know
8. (shower)   could   flood   flow
9. crow   bloom   (crown)   would

Reading Skills

1. Tatsu is sitting in the shade on the front steps because __it is a very__ __hot day__
2. Tatsu titles her drawing "Heat" because __the sun is what is__ __making her so hot__
3. Write **R** next to the sentences that tell about something real. Write **M** next to the sentences that are about made-up things.
   __M__ A person can make shade by drawing a picture of it.
   __M__ A person can draw a picture of heat.
   __R__ A person can draw a picture of the sun.

The **narrator** is the person who tells a story. Answer these questions.

4. Because the narrator is also a character, she uses the words *I* and *me* to tell her story. Find a place in the story where one of these words is used. Write the sentence here.
   __Answers will vary.__
5. Where in the story do you discover what the narrator's name is?
   __When her brother asks her a__
   __question.__

111

Page 113

Vocabulary Skills

Listen to the sound of the **c** in *cool*. Circle the words below that have the same sound as the **c** in *cool*.

1. (cover)   cereal
2. chin   (corner)
3. center   (coming)
4. cell   (clap)

When a short word has an **ing** ending, the syllable break comes between the word and its ending. So, *cooling* divides into *cool / ing*. For each word below, draw a line to divide the word into syllables.

5. build/ing
6. draw/ing
7. be/ing

Reading Skills

1. Why do Mario and Katie choose to draw pictures of cool water and a snow bank?
   __because it helps them think__
   __about being cool on a hot day__
2. Why does Tatsu cross out her own picture of the sun?
   __She thinks it might be__
   __making things feel hotter.__

3. Do you think that thinking about cool things can help a person cool down? Write why or why not.
   __Answers will vary.__
4. Can you remember a hot day? How did it feel? What did you do to cool down?
   __Answers will vary.__

Study Skills

Two sets of guide words from a dictionary are shown here in bold print. Beside each entry word below, write the page number on which it would be found.

chalk / check	p. 194
chew / chore	p. 201

1. chime __201__
2. chief __201__
3. chapter __194__
4. chive __201__
5. cheap __194__
6. chatter __194__
7. charm __194__
8. chimney __201__

113

Answer Key

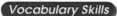

Page 115

Vocabulary Skills

Circle the correct letters to complete each word. Write the letters in the blank.

1. The stick burned in the f__ir__e.
   ar   er   (ir)

2. Did you know you were an __ar__tist?
   er   (ar)   ir

3. We think the pict__ur__es are quite well done.
   ir   or   (ur)

4. We adm__ir__e them very much.
   (ir)   ur   er

A **suffix** is a group of letters added to the end of a word that changes the meaning of the word. The suffix **-ful** means "full of." So, *joyful* means "full of joy."

Add **ful** to the words below. Use the new words to complete the sentences.

power	grace	care

5. The artists paid __careful__ attention to details.

6. The curving necks of the horses look very __graceful__.

7. The great size of one buffalo makes it look especially __powerful__.

Write a compound word using the underlined words in each sentence.

8. Some artists made <u>prints</u> of a <u>hand</u> on the wall.
   __handprints__

9. Did you <u>brush</u> the <u>paint</u> on with a stick?
   __paintbrush__

Reading Skills

1. This article is mostly about
   _____ animals that lived thousands of years ago.
   __X__ early cave art.
   _____ how early people survived.

2. What did early cave artists use for paint?
   __animal fat mixed with dirt or berries__

3. Where did early artists make their drawings?
   __on walls deep inside caves__

4. Early cave art has been found in more than __130__ caves.

5. How do you like the cave art shown on this page? How is it the same or different from other drawings you have seen of mammoths?
   __Answers will vary.__

115

Page 117

Vocabulary Skills

Form the plural of each word below by changing the **y** to **i** and adding **es**. Write the word on the line.

1. supply __supplies__
2. story __stories__
3. family __families__
4. bakery __bakeries__

Form a contraction from each pair of words. Write the contraction on the line.

5. do not __don't__
6. will not __won't__
7. can not __can't__
8. did not __didn't__

Reading Skills

1. Would you like to have a mural in your home? Write why or why not.
   __Answers will vary.__
   _____

2. Do you think the author wrote this article to make you laugh, give you information, or persuade you to do something?
   __to give information__

3. The author included some bold words in the article. She wanted readers to learn those words, so she included their meanings nearby. Find one of the words and look for its meaning. Write the word and its meaning here.
   __Answer should cite *mural*,__
   __*myths* or *mosaic*, along with its__
   __meaning from the article.__

Write the best word to complete each sentence below.

4. I would like a __picture__ of a garden on my wall. (jacket, picture, notebook)

5. The bread in the Roman __bakery__ mural looks yummy. (bakery, crown, sticky)

6. Would you like to use a million tiny __pieces__ to make a mosaic? (pieces, motions, signs)

Study Skills

Number each list of words below in alphabetical order.

1. __3__ story   2. __1__ ago
   __1__ picture   __2__ home
   __4__ world   __4__ whole
   __2__ scene   __3__ wall

117

Page 119

Vocabulary Skills

Use the words below to complete the sentences. You will use each word twice.

pen	spot

1. Please use a __pen__, not a pencil.

2. It's easy to __spot__ her; she's the only one with red hair.

3. Please put the dogs in their __pen__.

4. Oh, the ink made a __spot__ on my paper.

In each row below, circle the three words that belong together.

5. (letter) (postcard) desk (stamp)
6. (brother) (mother) (aunt) teacher
7. sky (sand) (stones) (rocks)
8. (beach) grass (hill) (mountain)

Add the ending **-ly** to each word. Use the new words to complete the sentences. If the base word ends in a consonant followed by **y**, change the **y** to **i**, then add **ly**.

eager	secret	easy

9. Lucy __easily__ thought of many things to say to Isabel.

10. She waits __eagerly__ for Isabel's letter.

11. Don't tell anyone that Lucy __secretly__ doesn't mind her red hair.

Reading Skills

1. The members of Lucy's family are __her father, mother, and__ __brother__.

2. What is Lucy's real name?
   __Lucinda__

3. Where does Lucy's pen pal live? How do you know?
   __In the Dominican Republic; Lucy__
   __wonders whether the water in South__
   __Carolina had come from there.__

4. What details do we learn about Lucy from her letter?
   __She has red hair; she is in third__
   __grade; she has two parents and__
   __a brother; she sings in a choir.__

5. What do you think will happen after Lucy finishes writing her letter?
   __Answers will vary.__
   _____
   _____

119

Page 121

Vocabulary Skills

Write the words from the article that have these meanings.

1. sloping sharply
   __steep__ Par. 1

2. always present; happening again and again
   __constant__ Par. 3

3. the uppermost part of a thing
   __surface__ Par. 5

When something happened in the past, add **ed** to the action word. Some words, however, do not follow that pattern.

Use each word pair to complete a sentence.

| shake—shook |
| grow—grew |
| find—found |

4. I will __find__ many shells today. Yesterday, I __found__ many also.

5. Does seaweed __grow__ in the water? Jan told me it __grew__ on the beach.

6. You can __shake__ this shell, but I __shook__ it already and didn't hear anything.

Reading Skills

1. What do beaches have in common?
   __They all have some kind__
   __of rock or stone material.__

2. Why do beaches have stones or sand on them?
   __The water, wind, rain, and frost break__
   __down rocks into smaller pieces.__

3. What causes waves?
   __wind__

4. Why does the article mention a rug?
   __The rug is an example of__
   __how a wave works.__

Study Skills

1. This article has two sections. What are they titled?
   __"The Beach" and "The__
   __Waves"__

2. If you were especially interested in water, what section would you look under?
   __The Waves__

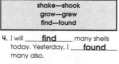

121

Answer Key

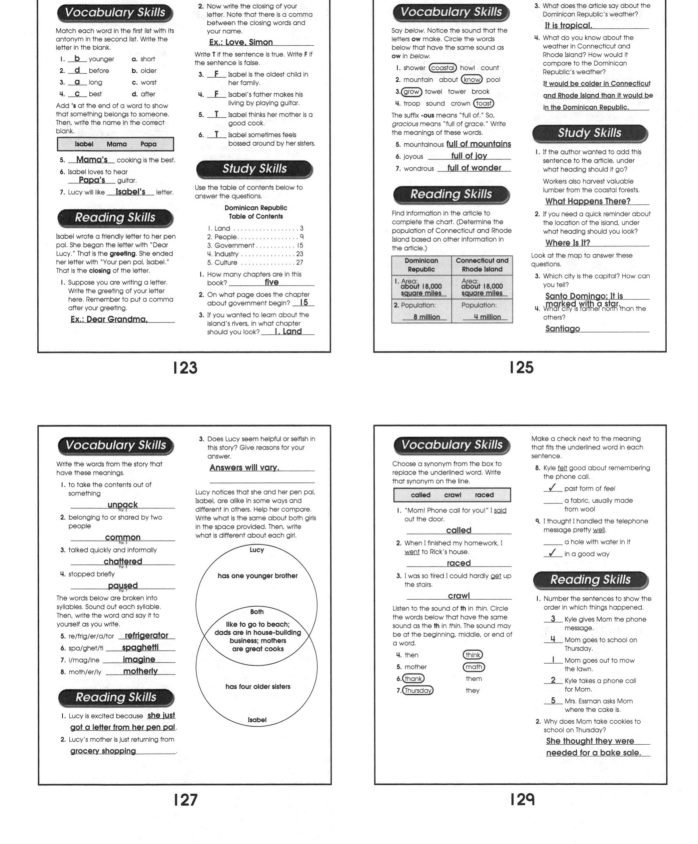

Page 123

Vocabulary Skills

Match each word in the first list with its antonym in the second list. Write the letter in the blank.

1. __b__ younger   a. short
2. __d__ before   b. older
3. __a__ long   c. worst
4. __c__ best   d. after

Add **'s** at the end of a word to show that something belongs to someone. Then, write the name in the correct blank.

| Isabel | Mama | Papa |

5. __Mama's__ cooking is the best.
6. Isabel loves to hear __Papa's__ guitar.
7. Lucy will like __Isabel's__ letter.

Reading Skills

Isabel wrote a friendly letter to her pen pal. She began the letter with "Dear Lucy." That is the **greeting**. She ended her letter with "Your pen pal, Isabel." That is the **closing** of the letter.

1. Suppose you are writing a letter. Write the greeting of your letter here. Remember to put a comma after your greeting.
   Ex.: Dear Grandma,

2. Now write the closing of your letter. Note that there is a comma between the closing words and your name.
   Ex.: Love, Simon

Write **T** if the sentence is true. Write **F** if the sentence is false.

3. __F__ Isabel is the oldest child in her family.
4. __F__ Isabel's father makes his living by playing guitar.
5. __T__ Isabel thinks her mother is a good cook.
6. __T__ Isabel sometimes feels bossed around by her sisters.

Study Skills

Use the table of contents below to answer the questions.

Dominican Republic
Table of Contents

1. Land 3
2. People 9
3. Government 15
4. Industry 23
5. Culture 27

1. How many chapters are in this book? __five__
2. On what page does the chapter about government begin? __15__
3. If you wanted to learn about the island's rivers, in what chapter should you look? __1, Land__

Page 125

Vocabulary Skills

Say *below*. Notice the sound that the letters **ow** make. Circle the words below that have the same sound as **ow** in *below*.

1. shower (coastal) howl count
2. mountain about (know) pool
3. (grow) towel tower brook
4. troop sound crown (toast)

The suffix **-ous** means "full of." So, *gracious* means "full of grace." Write the meanings of these words.

5. mountainous __full of mountains__
6. joyous __full of joy__
7. wondrous __full of wonder__

Reading Skills

Find information in the article to complete the chart. (Determine the population of Connecticut and Rhode Island based on other information in the article.)

	Dominican Republic	Connecticut and Rhode Island
1. Area:	about 18,000 square miles	about 18,000 square miles
2. Population:	8 million	4 million

3. What does the article say about the Dominican Republic's weather?
   It is tropical.

4. What do you know about the weather in Connecticut and Rhode Island? How would it compare to the Dominican Republic's weather?
   It would be colder in Connecticut and Rhode Island than it would be in the Dominican Republic.

Study Skills

1. If the author wanted to add this sentence to the article, under what heading should it go?
   Workers also harvest valuable lumber from the coastal forests.
   What Happens There?

2. If you need a quick reminder about the location of the island, under what heading should you look?
   Where Is It?

Look at the map to answer these questions.

3. Which city is the capital? How can you tell?
   Santo Domingo; It is marked with a star.

4. What city is farther north than the others?
   Santiago

Page 127

Vocabulary Skills

Write the words from the story that have these meanings.

1. to take the contents out of something
   __unpack__ _Par. 2_

2. belonging to or shared by two people
   __common__ _Par. 3_

3. talked quickly and informally
   __chattered__ _Par. 5_

4. stopped briefly
   __paused__ _Par. 7_

The words below are broken into syllables. Sound out each syllable. Then, write the word and say it to yourself as you write.

5. re/frig/er/a/tor __refrigerator__
6. spa/ghet/ti __spaghetti__
7. i/mag/ine __imagine__
8. moth/er/ly __motherly__

Reading Skills

1. Lucy is excited because __she just got a letter from her pen pal__.
2. Lucy's mother is just returning from __grocery shopping__.

3. Does Lucy seem helpful or selfish in this story? Give reasons for your answer.
   Answers will vary.

Lucy notices that she and her pen pal, Isabel, are alike in some ways and different in others. Help her compare. Write what is the same about both girls in the space provided. Then, write what is different about each girl.

- **Lucy**: has one younger brother
- **Both**: like to go to beach; dads are in house-building business; mothers are great cooks
- **Isabel**: has four older sisters

Page 129

Vocabulary Skills

Choose a synonym from the box to replace the underlined word. Write that synonym on the line.

| called | crawl | raced |

1. "Mom! Phone call for you!" I said out the door.
   __called__

2. When I finished my homework, I went to Rick's house.
   __raced__

3. I was so tired I could hardly get up the stairs.
   __crawl__

Listen to the sound of **th** in *thin*. Circle the words below that have the same sound as the **th** in *thin*. The sound may be at the beginning, middle, or end of a word.

4. then   (think)
5. mother   (math)
6. (thank)   them
7. (Thursday) they

Make a check next to the meaning that fits the underlined word in each sentence.

8. Kyle felt good about remembering the phone call.
   __✓__ past form of *feel*
   _____ a fabric, usually made from wool

9. I thought I handled the telephone message pretty well.
   _____ a hole with water in it
   __✓__ in a good way

Reading Skills

1. Number the sentences to show the order in which things happened.
   __3__ Kyle gives Mom the phone message.
   __4__ Mom goes to school on Thursday.
   __1__ Mom goes out to mow the lawn.
   __2__ Kyle takes a phone call for Mom.
   __5__ Mrs. Essman asks Mom where the cake is.

2. Why does Mom take cookies to school on Thursday?
   She thought they were needed for a bake sale.

Answer Key

Page 131

Vocabulary Skills

Write the words from the story that have these meanings.

1. happened or done again and again

   repeated

2. gave knowledge or skill to someone

   taught

3. failed to notice or do something

   overlooked

Circle the correct letters to complete each word. Write the letters in the blank.

4. What did you say to the p__er__son on the phone?

   ar   (er)   ir

5. What are the three basic p__ar__ts of a phone message?

   (ar)   ur   ir

6. I hope I pass the Phone Mann__er__s from Mom class.

   ur   ir   (er)

Reading Skills

1. What important parts of a phone message did Kyle forget the other day?

   All four parts—name, number, write it down, and deliver the message.

2. Look at the illustration. What do you think Mom is saying? Write the dialogue.

   Answers will vary.

Study Skills

You have just attended the Phone Manners from Mom class. How should you respond to these telephone situations?

1. The phone rings. You answer it by saying, " **Hello. (Last Name)** residence. This is (First Name) speaking."

2. Your dad is reading a book on the porch. The phone rings and the person says "May I speak to your father?" What do you say?

   Yes you may. May I ask who is calling, please?

3. Your mom is washing her hair and can't come to the phone. What are the four important parts of a phone message?

   name, number, write it down, deliver the message

Number the list of words below in alphabetical order.

4. __3__ telephone

   __1__ repeat

   __4__ tones

   __2__ speaking

131

Page 133

Vocabulary Skills

Abbreviations may be used to save time or space. Replace each underlined item in the message below with an abbreviation from the box.

a.m.	p.m.
Fri.	Wed.
Mon.	

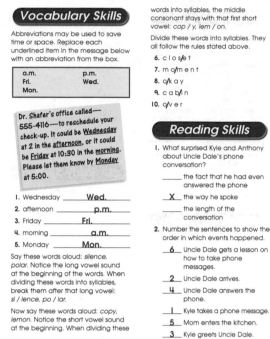

Dr. Shafer's office called—555-4116—to reschedule your check-up. It could be <u>Wednesday</u> at 2 in the <u>afternoon</u>, or it could be <u>Friday</u> at 10:30 in the <u>morning</u>. Please let them know by <u>Monday</u> at 5:00.

1. Wednesday **Wed.**

2. afternoon **p.m.**

3. Friday **Fri.**

4. morning **a.m.**

5. Monday **Mon.**

Say these words aloud: *silence, polar*. Notice the long vowel sound at the beginning of the words. When dividing these words into syllables, break them after that long vowel: si / lence, po / lar.

Now say these words aloud: *copy, lemon*. Notice the short vowel sound at the beginning. When dividing these

words into syllables, the middle consonant stays with that first short vowel: cop / y, lem / on.

Divide these words into syllables. They all follow the rules stated above.

6. c l o s/e t

7. m o/m e n t

8. o/k a y

9. c a b/i n

10. o/v e r

Reading Skills

1. What surprised Kyle and Anthony about Uncle Dale's phone conversation?

   _____ the fact that he had even answered the phone

   __X__ the way he spoke

   _____ the length of the conversation

2. Number the sentences to show the order in which events happened.

   __6__ Uncle Dale gets a lesson on how to take phone messages.

   __2__ Uncle Dale arrives.

   __4__ Uncle Dale answers the phone.

   __1__ Kyle takes a phone message.

   __5__ Mom enters the kitchen.

   __3__ Kyle greets Uncle Dale.

133

Page 135

Vocabulary Skills

In each row below, circle the three words that belong together.

1. wave (talk) (laugh) (sing)

2. (pal) (buddy) pest (friend)

3. (electricity) hearing (current) (wire)

Form the plural of each word below by adding **s**. Write the word on the line.

4. voice **voices**

5. telephone **telephones**

6. network **networks**

7. computer **computers**

8. wave **waves**

9. wire **wires**

Reading Skills

1. The article says it's not your voice, but **sound waves** made by your voice, that enter the telephone's microphone.

2. When the current in a telephone wire is flowing smoothly, what does the person on the other end hear?

   nothing

3. When sound waves interrupt the flow of current, what does the person on the other end hear?

   the speaker's voice

4. How long ago did people know that sound could travel along a wire?

   almost 400 years ago

5. How long ago did Alexander Graham Bell invent the telephone?

   about 130 years ago

Write **F** next to each sentence that is a fact. Write **O** next to each sentence that is an opinion.

6. __F__ Sound waves travel along a wire with the help of electrical current.

7. __O__ The telephone is the most important invention of the last 200 years.

8. __O__ Without the telephone, modern businesses would fail.

9. How do you and other members of your family use the telephone today?

   Answers will vary.

10. What would it be like if you had to get along without telephones? How else would you communicate?

   Answers will vary.

135

Page 137

Vocabulary Skills

Write the words from the story that have these meanings.

1. got comfortable

   snuggled

2. usual

   normal

3. singing with lips closed

   humming

4. container, usually made of glass

   jar

5. to coat something with a layer of something

   spread

These pairs of words sound the same, but have different meanings and spellings. Write the correct word from each pair to complete each sentence.

| heard—herd | sea—see |
| bare—bear | scent—sent |

6. The honey **bear** was full.

7. The heavy **scent** of flowers brought the bees.

8. She couldn't **see** the syrup in the fridge.

9. Lisa groaned when she **heard** there was no syrup.

Reading Skills

1. What clues tell you that the narrator is in bed? Write the words or phrases from the story.

   "snuggled under the covers"; "too close to sleep"

2. How do you know that having pancakes for breakfast must be a special thing?

   It says the smell of pancakes was not a normal smell.

3. The word that best describes this family is

   _____ rough.

   _____ noisy.

   __X__ pleasant.

Circle the name or word that each underlined word, or **pronoun**, stands for.

4. Mom said <u>she</u> was sure there was still some syrup.

   Lisa   syrup   (Mom)

5. When <u>he</u> heard the news, Dad offered to go to the store.

   store   (Dad)   news

6. Lisa waited quietly. <u>She</u> loved pancakes most of all.

   Mom   (Lisa)   pancakes

137

Answer Key

Page 139

Vocabulary Skills

Words whose meanings are opposite are called **antonyms**. Match each word in the first list with its antonym in the second list. Write the letter in the blank.

1. **b** old   a. sour
2. **d** light   b. young
3. **a** sweet   c. fresh
4. **c** spoiled   d. heavy

Form a contraction from each pair of words. Write the contraction on the line.

5. that is **that's**
6. was not **wasn't**
7. did not **didn't**
8. let us **let's**
9. do not **don't**
10. it is **it's**

Reading Skills

1. List the reasons the author gives for making honey our national food.

   Honey lasts pretty much forever.
   Honey is sweet.
   The bees would like it.
   Honey is useful.

2. Do you think those are good reasons for naming honey as a national food? Write why or why not.

   Answers will vary. _____
   _____

3. Sometimes, an author has more than one purpose for writing. What two purposes do you think this author had for writing the honey article?

   X to entertain readers
   _____ to give an explanation of honey bees' lives
   X to persuade readers that honey is good
   _____ to describe how honey resists bacteria

4. This article is mostly about

   X how good honey is.
   _____ the food value of honey.

Write the best word to complete each sentence below.

5. It's amazing that the honey didn't **spoil**. (burst, spoil, mend)
6. I like to **spread** honey on hot toast. (spread, clap, handle)
7. As bees **collect** nectar, they also spread pollen. (collect, enter, change)

139

Page 141

Vocabulary Skills

Add **ed** to an action word to show that something happened in the past. If the base word ends in a silent **e**, add only **d**.

Add **d** or **ed** to each word. Use the new words to complete the sentences.

turn	offer	raise
name		watch

1. Eliza wasn't singing, so Mr. Hamlin had **watched** her.
2. When she spoke, some students **turned** around and smiled.
3. Eliza thought the song was **named** after her.
4. As the song ended, Eliza **raised** her hand.
5. Natalie was the only one who **offered** an idea.

Some action words do not follow the usual pattern. Instead of adding **-ed** to show that something happened in the past, change the entire word.

Match each action word with its past form.

6. **e** give   a. sang
7. **d** think   b. drew
8. **b** draw   c. made
9. **a** sing   d. thought
10. **c** make   e. gave

Listen to the sound of **g** in *Georgie*. Circle the words below that have the same sound as the **g** in *Georgie*. The sound may be at the beginning, middle, or end of a word.

11. (energy)   giggle
12. good   (giant)
13. guess   (change)
14. (engine)   again

Reading Skills

1. Write **R** next to two sentences that tell about real things.

   R Anyone can make up a song.
   R A song can be happy or sad.
   _____ The words of a song are always true.

Study Skills

In what volume of the encyclopedia would you look to find these topics? Write the volume number.

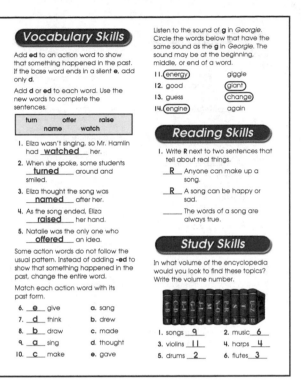

1. songs **9**   2. music **6**
3. violins **11**   4. harps **4**
5. drums **2**   6. flutes **3**

141

Page 143

Vocabulary Skills

Say *flow*. Notice the sound that the letters **ow** make. Circle the words below that have the same sound as **ow** in *flow*. The sound may come at the beginning, middle, or end of the word.

1. bound   you   course   (tow)
2. country   trouble   (throat)   vowel
3. around   two   (know)   countless
4. now   sound   voice   (follow)

Use the following words to form compound words. Then, use the compound words to complete the sentences.

battle		every
day		field

5. It was very sad to visit the **battlefield**.
6. Some folk songs recall the **everyday** tasks that people used to do.

Reading Skills

1. What is the difference between a ballad and a folk song?

   A ballad is longer and usually tells
   a story. A folk song is shorter and
   tells of a feeling or experience.

2. Why do you suppose someone wrote "Farewell, Nancy"?

   A sailor was leaving his wife
   or girlfriend to go to sea.

3. Why do you think someone would make a song about saying good-bye?

   Answers will vary. Ex.: It might
   help someone say good-bye.
   It might help when "Nancy" is
   missing the sailor

4. "When Johnny Comes Marching Home Again" is a well-known ballad. Even if you don't know the words, the title hints at the song's story. What do you think it is?

   Answers will vary but may
   mention a soldier coming
   home from war.

Study Skills

Number each list of words below in alphabetical order.

1. **3** settlers   2. **4** wrote
   1 folk   **1** war
   2 music   **3** write
   4 songs   **2** words

143

Page 145

Vocabulary Skills

Circle the word that is a synonym of the underlined word or words in each sentence.

1. Grandpa had a meal <u>ready</u> when Grandma came in from the field.

   extra   silent   (prepared)

2. The boys did not want to <u>alter</u> their lunch habits.

   (change)   refresh   outlive

3. Grandpa's farm called for a lot of hard <u>work</u>.

   attempt   mistrust   (labor)

Add **'s** at the end of a word to show that something belongs to someone. Add **'s** to each name. Then, write the name in the correct blank.

A.J.	Grandpa	Max

4. **Grandpa's** sandwich was delicious.
5. Max washed his brother **A.J.'s** apple.
6. Grandma added peanut butter to **Max's** sandwich.

Circle the correct letters to complete each word. Write the letters in the blank.

7. Grandma and Grandpa are f **ar** mers.

   er   (ar)   ir

8. Grandma had to drive the tract **or**.

   ar   (or)   er

9. Grandma's lips c **ur** ved in a little smile.

   er   ir   (ur)

Reading Skills

1. What do Grandma and Grandpa do for a living?

   They are farmers.

2. Do you think Grandma likes peanut butter? Why?

   Ex.: Yes, because she liked
   the sandwich Grandpa made.

3. How do you like the sound of a peanut butter-bacon-banana sandwich?

   Answers will vary. _____
   _____
   _____

4. What do you think will happen next?

   Answers will vary. _____
   _____
   _____

145

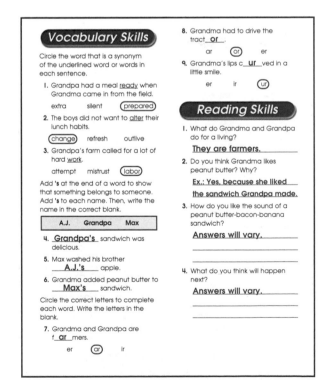

Answer Key

Answer Key

Vocabulary Skills

Write the words from the article that have these meanings.

1. between the ages of 13 and 19

   teenager Par. 2

2. given a job

   hired Par. 2

3. serious study

   research Par. 3

4. changes or additions that make something better

   improvements Par. 3

5. make money

   profit Par. 5

Form a contraction from each pair of words. Write the contraction on the line.

6. there is **there's**

7. did not **didn't**

8. he would **he'd**

9. who will **who'll**

10. they are **they're**

The words below are broken into syllables. Sound out each syllable. Then, write the word and say it to yourself as you write.

11. ag/ri/cul/ture **agriculture**

12. im/prove/ments **improvements**

13. in/ven/tions **inventions**

14. sci/en/tists **scientists**

Reading Skills

1. This article is mostly about

   X Carver's work with peanuts.

   _____ Carver's fame as a scientist.

   _____ Carver's fight to get an education.

2. George Washington Carver lived from **1864** until **1943**.

3. While in college, he studied **agriculture**, which is the study of **farming**.

4. Carver made hundreds of products from peanuts. List some that the article mentions.

   Answers will vary.

5. Which of the products seems the most interesting or the most unusual to you? Write why.

   Answers will vary.

Write F next to each sentence that is a fact. Write O next to each sentence that is an opinion.

6. **O** Carver saved Southern farmers from ruining the land.

7. **F** Planting peanuts after cotton keeps the soil healthy.

8. **O** Carver is America's greatest black scientist.

147

Vocabulary Skills

These pairs of words sound the same, but have different meanings. Write the correct word from each pair to complete each sentence.

rap—wrap	two—too
wood—would	great—grate

1. I wonder if you **would** reach the paint for me.

2. We have only **two** rubber stamps to use.

3. If you need me, just **rap** on my office door.

4. That noise is really starting to **grate** on my nerves.

Say *because* aloud. Notice the long vowel sound at the beginning of the word. When dividing this word into syllables, break it after the long vowel: *be / cause*.

Now, say *present*, which means "a gift." Notice the short vowel sound at the beginning. When dividing this word into syllables, the middle consonant stays with the first short vowel: *pres / ent*.

Divide these words into syllables. They all follow the rules stated above.

5. o t h/e r

6. e/n o u g h

7. e a/g e r

8. p a/p e r

9. n e v/e r

Reading Skills

Write the best word to complete each sentence below.

1. Stephanie and her mom look for a box in the **attic**. (attic, entrance, ending)

2. Stephanie was proud that she had **built** her present. (waved, built, filled)

3. Stephanie was **curious** about Mom's wrapping idea. (clever, crazy, curious)

Circle the name or word that each underlined word, or **pronoun**, stands for.

4. Mom said <u>she</u> had an idea for wrapping paper.

   idea (Mom) Stephanie

5. When <u>she</u> heard the idea, Stephanie was doubtful.

   idea Mom (Stephanie)

6. Mom was all ready. <u>She</u> had already set out the supplies.

   supplies (Mom) Stephanie

Study Skills

Number the group of words below in alphabetical order.

1. **1** answer   **4** present

   2 birdhouse   **3** great

149

Vocabulary Skills

Form the plural of each word below by adding **s**, **es**, or by changing **y** to **i** and adding **es**. Write the word on the line.

1. design **designs**

2. supply **supplies**

3. paintbrush **paintbrushes**

4. stamp **stamps**

5. box **boxes**

The prefix **multi-** means "many" or "much." The prefix **micro-** means "small" or "short." Combine one of these prefixes with each word in the box. Then, use the new words to complete the sentences.

colored	scope
film	millionaire

6. I looked at old newspapers at the library on the **microfilm** machine.

7. My design will be bright and **multicolored**.

8. This fossil is so small you need a **microscope** to see it.

9. I'll start a stamp printing company and become a **mutimillionaire**

Reading Skills

1. The author used a numbered list for the instructions. Why do you think this was done?

   Answers will vary.

2. What other kinds of instructions, with numbered lists, have you seen?

   Answers will vary.

3. Number the sentences to show the order in which to complete the stamping project.

   3 Dip stamp into paint.

   4 Press stamp on paper.

   1 Put paint in plastic lids.

   6 Let dry.

   2 Lay out sheet of paper.

   5 Lift the stamp.

4. Why do the instructions say you should put small amounts of paint in plastic lids?

   So you can dip stamps easily.

5. What can you think of that you would like to decorate with stamps?

   Answers will vary.

151

Notes

Notes

Notes

Notes